Counseling
Before
Marriage

RESOURCES FOR
CHRISTIAN COUNSELING

RESOURCES FOR CHRISTIAN COUNSELING

1. Innovative Approaches to Counseling *Gary R. Collins*
2. Counseling Christian Workers *Louis McBurney*
3. Self-Talk, Imagery, and Prayer in Counseling
   H. Norman Wright
4. Counseling Those with Eating Disorders
   Raymond E. Vath
5. Counseling the Depressed *Archibald D. Hart*
6. Counseling for Family Violence and Abuse
   Grant L. Martin
7. Counseling in Times of Crisis
   Judson J. Swihart and Gerald C. Richardson
8. Counseling and Guilt *Earl D. Wilson*
9. Counseling and the Search for Meaning *Paul R. Welter*
10. Counseling for Unplanned Pregnancy and Infertility
    Everett L. Worthington, Jr.
11. Counseling for Problems of Self-Control
    Richard P. Walters
12. Counseling for Substance Abuse and Addiction
    Stephen Van Cleave, Walter Byrd, Kathy Revell
13. Counseling and Self-Esteem *David E. Carlson*
14. Counseling Families *George A. Rekers*
15. Counseling and Homosexuality *Earl D. Wilson*
16. Counseling for Anger *Mark P. Cosgrove*
17. Counseling and the Demonic *Rodger K. Bufford*
18. Counseling and Divorce *David A. Thompson*
19. Counseling and Marriage *DeLoss D. and Ruby M. Friesen*
20. Counseling the Sick and Terminally Ill *Gregg R. Albers*
21. Counseling Adult Children of Alcoholics
    Sandra D. Wilson
22. Counseling and Children *Warren Byrd and Paul Warren*
23. Counseling Before Marriage *Everett L. Worthington, Jr.*

(Other volumes forthcoming)

VOLUME TWENTY-THREE

Counseling
Before
Marriage

EVERETT L. WORTHINGTON, Jr., Ph.D.

RESOURCES FOR
CHRISTIAN COUNSELING

— General Editor —

Gary R. Collins, Ph.D.

WORD PUBLISHING
Dallas · London · Sydney · Singapore

Library of Congress Cataloging-in-Publication Data

Worthington, Everett L., 1946–
    Counseling before marriage / Everett L. Worthington, Jr.
        p.   cm. — (Resources for Christian counseling)
    Includes bibliographical references.
    ISBN 0-8499-0592-3 :
    1. Marriage counseling. 2. Pastoral counseling. 3. Marriage—
    Religious aspects—Christianity. I. Title. II. Series.
    BV4012.27.W667   1990
    253.5—dc20   90-31340
                                             CIP

Printed in the United States of America

01239 AGF 987654321

In Memory of
ELW

CONTENTS

EDITOR'S PREFACE

THE WRITER OF THE OLD TESTAMENT BOOK of Ecclesiastes (probably King Solomon) clearly was a wise man. Near the beginning of his writing (Eccles. 1:9, 10) he wrote that "there is nothing new under the sun. Is there anything of which one can say, 'Look! This is something new'? It was here already, long ago; it was here before our time" (NIV). Then, near the end of his little book, the writer drops in this powerful sentence: "Of making many books there is no end, and much study wearies the body" (Eccles. 12:12 NIV).

One could argue, I suppose, that Solomon was kept so busy with his seven hundred wives and three hundred concubines that he had no time to read many books or to keep up with what might have been new. It also is unlikely that he worried much about getting counseling before marriage and remarriage.

Even so, I sometimes think about the words of Ecclesiastes when I go into a bookstore. Shelf after shelf is lined with books that deal with the same topics, give much of the same information, and are written by many of the same authors. In Christian circles, some topics appear with disturbing frequency; near the top of this list are books on marriage and the family. These are poured from the presses in great numbers but apart from the illustrations and anecdotes, we seldom seem to read anything fresh or "new under the sun."

Some of this was in my mind as I looked for an author who could bring a fresh perspective to the old but important topic of premarital counseling. When I asked Everett Worthington, his reply was immediate.

"I don't believe in traditional premarital counseling," he said.

"Good!" I replied without hesitation. "You obviously are the right guy to write the book."

It took longer for Dr. Worthington to agree and, as his introduction notes, the task has not been easy. Books on premarital counseling have tended to advocate lengthy, time-consuming, somewhat inflexible approaches that may be creative and well-intentioned, but often are introduced too late (when the couple is well along with wedding plans). Rarely do authors modify their approaches to include premarital counseling with people who have been married before. The writers assume that premarital counseling is beneficial, but research is sparse, often showing no awareness of what the existing research might indicate.

Everett Worthington, in contrast, has done his homework, has shared what research shows about the effectiveness of premarital counseling, and has given a variety of guidelines that can be helpful in working with couples. Furthermore, he has been sensitive to the uniqueness of each couple who comes to be married. This is more than a book on individual and group approaches to premarital counseling; it summarizes what we know about preparation for and adjustment to both marriage and remarriage. The author gives no rigid formula for premarital counseling, but he offers a host of practical suggestions for developing approaches that acknowledge the uniqueness of each couple and each individual.

Like the other volumes in the Resources for Christian Counseling series, this book is intended to be practical and helpful. Written by counseling experts, each of whom has a strong Christian commitment and extensive counseling experience, the books are meant to be examples of accurate psychology and careful use of Scripture. Each is intended to have a clear evangelical perspective, careful documentation, a strong practical orientation, and freedom from the sweeping statements and undocumented rhetoric that sometimes characterize writing in the counseling field. Our goal is to provide books that are clearly written, useful, up-to-date overviews of the issues faced by contemporary Christian counselors—including pastoral counselors. All of the Resources for Christian Counseling books have similar bindings and together they are intended to comprise a helpful encyclopedia of Christian counseling.

Everett Worthington's earlier book, *Counseling for Unplanned Pregnancy and Infertility,* has been well received and, in my opinion, is one of the best in the series. The present volume is no less innovative and helpful. Dr. Worthington's earlier contributions to marriage counseling, lay counseling, counselor education, and counseling research have now been enhanced by a truly unique volume on premarital counseling. Those who know Ev Worthington will not be surprised. He is a humble and gracious man who is a diligent researcher, a highly respected professor, a competent therapist, and a careful writer. More important are his commitment to Christ and involvement with his family. As "icing on the cake" he has a delightful sense of humor, which spills into the pages of this book on occasion.

Ecclesiastes is right: it does seem that there is no end to the making of books—many of which contain "nothing new." But occasionally a volume comes along that is unique and refreshing. I hope you will agree that this new book fits that description.

Gary R. Collins, Ph.D.
Kildeer, Illinois

INTRODUCTION

COUNSELING AMID CONTROVERSY

OF ALL THE WRITING I'VE EVER DONE, I have had the hardest time with this book. I have blamed everyone from Gary Collins to George Bush, and everything from my responsibilities at school to global political tensions for the difficulties I've felt in writing it.

I recently attended a workshop on brief psychodynamic psychotherapy (which I had mistakenly thought to be videotapes of Freud doing psychoanalysis in his underwear). One case covered in the workshop involved the treatment of a woman beset with habitual procrastination. The therapist and client ultimately identified the problem as the woman's fear of rejection.

Although I typically am not troubled by procrastination, I saw that my difficulties in writing this book had a lot to do with my expectation that a book on divorce and remarriage might not be well received within the Christian community. Such feelings were strengthened anytime I had been involved in or observed a discussion of divorce or remarriage. Almost always, I saw controversy and division. Adrenaline levels quickly became elevated. Hurt feelings and arguments were common.

Disagreements abound over the theology of divorce and remarriage and the practice of counseling the divorced and re-married. Mostly, arguments over divorce and remarriage involve some amount of self-justification. If we preach or teach on divorce or remarriage, we take a public stand. If we have a loved one who has divorced, we feel compassion and want him or her to be able to remarry. Thus, we may justify that position using Scripture. If we counsel divorced people to help them deal with their pain, we may justify our expenditure of time and energy by the theological position we take.

I am not immune to such self-justification. I have taken public stands about divorce and remarriage, counseled married couples who have, despite my and their efforts, decided to divorce, and counseled remarried families. I have taught classes about the pain and difficulty of divorce and remarriage, and I've even seen the anguish of divorce within my family of origin. That Kirby and I, by God's grace, have had almost twenty happy years of marriage only heightens my empathy for those who have had to deal with the trauma of a severed relationship and the adjustment to new relationships during remarriage.

Also, I am plagued with indwelling sin that wants to honor myself and have my way, often more than I want to have God's way, regrettably. Undoubtedly, I sometimes misinterpret Scripture. None of us approaches Scripture without bias. We sometimes shape theology to conform with the often not-understood forces that may pressure us from within and without.

My theological background has undoubtedly influenced my own presuppositions. Raised in a Southern Baptist home, I fell away from my upbringing during my college years. In graduate school in nuclear engineering, I attended Roman Catholic mass for over a year with a roommate from Puerto Rico. In the Navy in California, I was invited to a Lutheran church, where I accepted Jesus as my savior and was baptized. I became heavily influenced by the writings of C. S. Lewis and Francis Schaeffer, and after I was released from active military service, Kirby and I briefly visited the L'Abri fellowship in

Switzerland. During graduate school in counseling psychology, I attended an Evangelical Free Church in Columbia, Missouri. Moving to Richmond, Virginia, after graduate school, Kirby and I joined a Presbyterian Church, where we stay today.

Even though I know that denominational labels often divide, I mention my own background because it should give you some understanding of my biases. I value the variety of traditions in Christendom and find them useful correctives to each other's excesses and deficits.

Throughout the writing of this book, I have hoped that it would contribute to healing rather than hurting among people dealing with the practicalities of divorce and remarriage. As the book has progressed, though, I have seen that however I portray the issues, people will always disagree.

I believe that the counselor, although he or she might have clear ideas about the rightness or wrongness of remarriage (which may even be shared in a non-coercive way with the couple), must stress to the couple that divorce and remarriage are complex theological and practical issues and that each couple must examine the Scriptures and their consciences before God to determine his will for them. However, that approach falls afoul of people on both sides of the issue who believe Scripture to be absolutely clear about the issue and whose churches might have an established policy about remarriage.

Nonetheless, I believe that there is not 100 percent clarity within Scripture on the issues of divorce and remarriage, though some things *are* clearly specified. Larry Christenson once pointed out that when God quickens a truth for us, we are often quick to turn that truth around and wallop our neighbor with the blunt end of it. We must carefully avoid that and consider each circumstance within the context of speaking the truth in love.

We seem always destined to walk the balance beam between justice and mercy with slippery feet that sweep us off on one side or the other—condemning when we should pardon and forgiving when we should stand firm for the truth. It is my hope that we will ever more frequently maintain our balance. We should strive for marital commitment and fidelity, and stand firm that "God hates divorce." This is always true, even when the marriage is abusive and harmful for both partners and children. The finding by a divorced person that remarriage brings substantial happiness relative to a previous marriage does not alter God's hatred for divorce. It merely means that he gives us "beauty for ashes [and] the oil of joy for mourning" (Isa. 61:3, KJV). It means that "in everything, God works for good with those who love him, who are called according to his purpose" (Rom. 8:28, RSV).

If you counsel the engaged-to-be-married or the engaged-to-be-remarried, I hope you can benefit from the practical information about marriage, divorce, and remarriage throughout this book. I also hope you can use some of the practical recommendations for counseling the engaged couple presented here. I hope you will examine your own understandings of marriage and remarriage and will arrive at a deeper knowledge of your positions on these issues. Hopefully, this knowledge can benefit your parishioners, clients, or counselees. Finally, I pray you will be able to put aside any theological differences between us and use whatever is appropriate from this work.

CHAPTER ONE

NOT JUST COUNSELING,
BUT *EFFECTIVE* COUNSELING

WHEN I TOLD ONE LOCAL PASTOR that I intended to write a book on premarriage counseling, his eyes rolled up in his head and his lip curled upward on one side.

"That's just what the world needs," he said, "one more premarital counseling program." He put on the patient look he probably uses with wayward children and said, "Look, I have books telling me how to do about three types of premarital counseling. Each one specifies 413 steps and 23 crucial marriage issues. Can I follow those prescriptions? Nope. Two weeks ago, two members of my congregation wanted me to marry them. I said that I required counseling with those whom I married. They reluctantly agreed to come to counseling and almost fell asleep during the first session. When I gave them some homework to complete between the first and second sessions, the guy looked at me as if I had just told him to wear starched underwear for a week."

I understood the pastor's feelings."Do you remember the commercial about ten years ago for Listerine?'' I asked him. "It said, 'I hate it, but I use it—twice a day.' That's the way I feel about most premarital counseling programs. We use them—probably because it sounds like they ought to work—but they often don't seem very satisfying either to us or to the couples we counsel."

This pastor's and my concerns about premarital counseling programs prompted this book. In the United States, several states require premarital counseling for minors.[1] In the Roman Catholic Church, premarital counseling is often required. In fact, the *Washington Post* (April 8, 1989) reports that 29 percent of Roman Catholics have had some formal preparation for marriage. Most of it takes place in large groups. In Protestant churches, many pastors will not marry congregants without counseling them first. Overall, the popularity of premarital counseling is high.

Most premarital counseling is done by clergy.[2] However, with recent legal requirements in states such as Ohio and California that minors have premarital counseling, a large number of mental health professionals also conduct programs.

Undoubtedly more people are counseled premaritally in some form each year than are counseled by psychotherapists. Yet, surprisingly little research has investigated whether premarital counseling is even effective.

Probably the fairest, up-to-the-minute evaluation of the effectiveness of premarital counseling programs is that they are thought to be effective to the extent that they (1) have clear goals, (2) last at least six to twelve weeks, (3) focus on communication and problem solving about issues that the couple considers relevant, and (4) include information, interaction between partners (especially with feedback by video or by other people), and discussion. Purely information-oriented approaches and time-constrained conjoint sessions might be effective; but there is no research to support that method.

While all these components are important and deserve careful attention by the counselor as he or she sets up a premarital counseling program, for brevity, in this chapter I'll consolidate these issues into four general topics: goals, timing, priorities, and practical considerations.

GOALS

Usually the goals of counseling are jointly derived between the counselor and the client. However, those goals are affected by the counseling setting, as well as the theoretical orientation of the counselor. One study found that counselors in secular counseling settings held different goals for their clients than did counselors in explicitly religious settings, such as pastoral counseling agencies.[3] And clients often set different goals for themselves when they go to an explicitly religious counselor, rather than to a secular counselor.

To establish the goals for premarital counseling, you should understand several things.

1. Consider what you think the outcome of premarital counseling ought to be.

2. Understand your own assumptions about potential problems in marriage and about how they can be avoided.

3. Understand the theories on which your counseling is based, which can alert you to possible inconsistencies in your goals.

What's the Desired Outcome?

Belinda and Randolph want premarital counseling. They say they are deeply in love. You know that Belinda has a history of short-term sexual relationships with several men, most of whom have been wealthy and have spent money lavishly on her. Randolph is insecure and has little experience with women. Although he is bright, he seems to have little awareness that Belinda may not be sincere in her professed love for him. What outcome would you like to see as a result of your premarital counseling with Belinda and Randolph?

This case illustrates some of the fundamental decisions required in premarital counseling. Should the counseling be aimed at helping a couple break up or get along together?

Should the couple be helped to make a "more realistic" appraisal of the situation, and if so, whose realism is to be used? Is the "realistic" view expected to help the man and woman decide to call off the marriage, or is it expected to alert them to potential difficulties they can either work on before or after marriage?

Consider the case of Paulette and Jason. They are twenty-three and twenty-five, respectively, well established in their careers, and psychologically well matched for each other. They both provide life and enthusiasm in the congregation. They have dated for three years and their relationship has grown progressively more mature. They seem ideal candidates for a lasting marriage. What would you like to see happen as a result of your premarital counseling with them? Would you like to see them understand each other better? Or would you like to help them acquire and demonstrate the abilities to solve the problems that characterize almost any marriage relationship? Do you believe that if they understand the potential problems, they will be able to solve or even avoid them? Or do you believe that understanding is not sufficient, that they could benefit by feedback into their actual practice of discussing differences and resolving conflicts?

Consider a third case. Marcia is thirty-four years old. A year ago, Claude, her husband of eleven years, was killed in an automobile accident, leaving her with three boys ages seven, five, and two. She has spent a year of emotional turmoil trying to get her life together while providing good parenting for the boys. About six months after Claude's death, she met Maurice, a twenty-six-year-old engineer. His attitudes are more liberal than you assess Marcia's to be. Further, his parents are of low socioeconomic status (SES) and he is employed at a considerably lower SES than was Marcia's first husband.

Despite the differences in Marcia's and Maurice's life experiences and circumstances, they appear mature and ready for marriage. Statistically, the deck is stacked in favor of a divorce; but they love each other and appear to be entering marriage with open eyes. What would you like to see happen as a result of premarital counseling? Would you like to dissuade, encourage, or remain neutral about their marital prospects? Would you want them to discuss likely areas of conflict, such as childrearing responsibilities, or would you focus on daily communication, understanding, empathy, and self-disclosure? Would you want them to improve their current relationship, or to focus on skills that might lessen the chances of divorce?

In each of these cases, your answers to the questions depend on both your assessment of the couple's likely future and on your beliefs about potential causes of and cures for marital difficulties.

Assumptions About Problems in Marriage

Although there are numerous theories of personality, marriage, and marital problems, the fundamental assumptions underlying these theories are limited. These two have most frequently governed the goals of premarital counseling programs:

1. *Healthy individuals make happy marriages.* "Healthy" individuals may be defined differently in various theories of counseling. For example, the psychoanalyst might define a healthy individual as one who is aware of and exerts ego control over his or her unconscious impulses and conflicts. The humanistic counselor, such as Rogers, or existential counselors, might describe the healthy individual as being aware of his or her feelings, thoughts, and behaviors, having high self-esteem, and relating well to others. For the cognitive counselor, the happy individual holds few irrational assumptions or beliefs, uses few maladaptive cognitive processes, does not engage in negative self-talk or self-instruction, has realistic expectations about self, partner, and marriage, and has a positive philosophy of life.

Counselors who hold the assumption that healthy individuals make healthy marriages will strive to help partners become self-aware (of whatever is thought to be responsible for good health) and to be aware of the needs and motivations of their partners. Some concession is made to the *interaction* of two individuals, but the interaction is generally thought to be a product of two individuals' *behaviors.*

2. *Relationships are the unique product of two people's communications.* How people communicate is a result of their past. Most people are thought to be capable of good communication.

5

But some partners form poor communication habits with each other because they are not rewarded for good communication or are punished for it.

Therapists who believe that communication *habits* are more important than individuals' *abilities* to communicate cite research to support their views. Married partners who have relationship difficulties have been consistently found to engage in relationship-destructive communication with their spouses but relationship-enhancing communication with opposite-sex strangers.[4] Their communication with their spouses is merely knee-jerk, habitual communication.

Counselors who hold the relationship-oriented assumption will sometimes teach couples new behaviors or new information. Mostly they try to break up the habit patterns and get the man and woman to communicate as well with each other as they know how to communicate with others. The couple will usually practice solving problems or negotiating conflict with the therapist's help.

TIMING

In premarital programs, intervention occurs all along the time line of relationship development. Despite family life education within the public schools (often beginning in early elementary grades), and despite the family orientation of most churches, many people arrive at the brink of marriage with misconceptions about it.

When is the optimal time for people to learn about married life so that knowledge can be most constructively applied to their own marriage relationship? Schumm and Denton have argued that couples are the most receptive to intervention *after* marriage,[5] and other reviewers have agreed with their assessment.[6] The argument for doing neomarital counseling rather than premarital counseling suggests that before marriage, couples are too romantically involved to face potential difficulties. They have decided to marry; to admit that problems might occur in marriage threatens that decision. Further, immediately after marriage, people are in the "honeymoon" period when they tend to overlook differences. This honeymoon period might last any time from five minutes after the ceremony to about six months after marriage, when, most authorities agree, the newlyweds begin to experience some tensions and difficulties that require resolution. Postponing the counseling until after this honeymoon period may inhibit a couple's participation in any *standardized* counseling program, because by that time spouses have too many issues specific to their relationship and do not want to spend time on issues they are not actively trying to resolve. So the optimal time to do effective counseling might be after the first few months of marriage but before the sixth month of marriage.[7]

It should be noted, however, that this reasoning is generally based on a *remedial* model for counseling, especially if the counselor waits later than six months. A *preventive* model of counseling would suggest that couples who receive powerful training *prior* to marriage might be able to avoid some of the adjustments that typically occur at the end of the honeymoon period. The crucial aspect of the preventive model is that the couple realize that the program plans for the future rather than relieves current strains. If the counselor can't convince the couple that the training is relevant, then the couple will likely complain—as did participants in Guldner's study—that the counselor seems to be looking for problems that do not really exist.[8]

PRIORITIES

How you design a premarital counseling program will reflect your own values and priorities. Where will your emphases be? Almost all effective premarital programs require couples to interact with each other and receive feedback, either from trainers or from other couples within the program (or both). However, the amount of time that is spent on the actual behavioral rehearsal and the type and amount of feedback differ widely across programs. In the Markman et al. program, almost the entire time is devoted to teaching behavioral skills or applying them.[9] In other programs, such as the Minnesota Couples Communication Program, more information is given and relatively much less time is taken up by couples communicating with each other and receiving feedback on their communication. Still other programs might have couples communicate but not give feedback about how they might improve their communication.[10]

What you emphasize will depend on what you think is important to help couples learn. It depends on your values.

PRACTICAL CONSIDERATIONS FOR COUNSELORS AND COUPLES

Not every pastor or mental health professional can afford to create or use well-researched premarital counseling programs of proven effectiveness. Also, most pastors are not trained to do premarital counseling, although they generally have done a lot of it. Thus, the quality of their counseling is highly variable. There is evidence that some pastors do not counsel well. To the contrary, though, there is substantial evidence that most parishioners are satisfied with the counseling they receive from their pastors.[11]

Some seminaries have begun to train pastors in marital and premarital counseling.[12] Even with this training, however, most pastors only know one style of premarital counseling, which reduces their ability to adapt the counseling to the needs of the couples they counsel. Furthermore, much of the pastors' teaching on preparation for marriage is theological. Even if the pastor values some of the discoveries of psychology, it is difficult for most to keep abreast of modern psychological theory and research.

From the couple's point of view, the mental health professional who is not employed by a church (and often even counselors who *are*) will usually charge a fee for services. This cost might be prohibitive for some couples, especially minor-age couples required by law to have premarital counseling. They are generally the least able to afford to pay it. If such couples are not covered by state funds or insurance (and premarital counseling is almost never considered a medical problem), the couple will generally select the counseling that is least expensive and still fulfills legal requirements. Unfortunately, that often means short, information-oriented programs, which are probably the least effective.

Decisions about goals, timing, priorities, and practical considerations are generally most effective when they are individualized according to the counselor and couples involved. We must avoid trying to force the couple into a mold that we have predetermined to be ideal. By failing to recognize each couple's uniqueness, we limit them, making negative feelings, rebellion, and conflict more likely. *As a counselor, I want to treat couples as people who can legitimately have different values and styles of life than I value.* My design of a premarital counseling program should reflect this. However, if the couple's lifestyle or values are in such conflict with my view of Scripture that I in good conscience cannot condone them, then I explain my views and give the couple the option of selecting a different counselor.

CHAPTER TWO

THE DEVELOPING RELATIONSHIP

SOMETIMES I CATCH MYSELF thinking that all couples preparing for marriage have the same needs—to share their values and expectations, to enjoy the romanticism and idealism while being open to learning how to resolve inevitable conflicts, and to be open to counseling if problems arise. In my saner moments, I remember couples I know, and I realize that such thinking is too simplistic.

For example, James and Caroline had been married thirty-five years. "The deepest thought James ever had was wondering what was for dinner," Caroline said. They both laughed. There was a sense of comfort and good humor between them that was almost palpable. "You know something, though? It doesn't bother us. The deepest thought *I* ever had was where we might go on vacation."

James looked around their comfortable living room. "Yeah, we're happy. We just don't talk about philosophy and such things much. Actually, I think it's boring. Now, don't get me wrong. I'm glad you folks at the university are interested in stuff like that, but it doesn't seem to make much difference to us."

Two other friends, Karen and Timothy, married sixteen years, claimed they had never had arguments or conflicts. Karen insisted they simply agreed on the basic values of life. "Well, maybe a few times we might disagree for a few minutes," she conceded. "But never about anything that matters."

What surprised me was that neither Karen nor Timothy was a stranger to conflict. Both were involved in school politics, as a past-president of the PTA and as a county school board commissioner. Both at times had stood resolutely for their beliefs against opposition. Yet they seemed to avoid conflict with each other.

On the other hand, Rod and Frankie, married twelve years, said life just wouldn't be the same without conflict. "We stomp through the house, yell at each other, and sometimes swear," said Frankie. "We've always been like that. We fight tough. We talk serious. And we love hard. It seems to make life worth living."

Each couple is a different novel. Some have similar plots; some are of the same genre. But each has its own story.

When we design programs to help couples prepare for marriage, or to help them repair damaged marriages, we would like to create programs that will appeal to everyone. That never works completely. A better way is to remember these three points:

1. Relationships develop in predictable ways, but . . .
2. No couple is perfectly predictable. All deviate from our idea of a blueprint of relationship development.
3. Nonetheless, by understanding how a typical relationship develops, we can counsel more effectively.

In this chapter we will briefly study the forces that lead two people to marriage. In the following chapters we'll look briefly at theology, sociology and psychology—the forces that shape a marriage.

How Relationships Develop

We usually expect that relationships will proceed along an ever-increasing path of deeper commitment, culminating in marriage.[1] These steps are outlined in Figure 2–1: attraction, dating, steady dating, engagement, and marriage. Sometimes cohabitation is a step in this pathway, too.

Huston et al. showed that this is only one of the ways relationships proceed toward marriage.[2] When newly married couples recalled the events of their courtship, the couples described passing through the traditional steps at various speeds. Some progressed steadily and rapidly in harmony; others moved slowly *or* rapidly, but with discord and turbulence just prior to the marriage. Still others moved with an uneven, jerky, on-again, off-again relationship in which the future of the relationship was often uncertain.

Describing relationship development by the traditional method tells little about what actually happens as relationships develop. Ira Reiss described the deepening relationship as a wheel that might turn several times before it is mature. There were four spokes to the wheel: rapport, self-revelation, mutual dependency, and personality need fulfillment.[3]

According to this theory, initially, couples achieve some sort of rapport, usually based on perceived similarities. After establishing rapport, partners share aspects of themselves. If each partner accepts the other's self-revelations, the couple might move to mutual dependency, in which the man and woman reward each other, listening to each other, sharing sexual intimacies, and pursuing leisure activities together. Finally, each partner may realize that his or her personality needs—to love, to be loved, to be trusted, to be encouraged in his or her ambition, and others—are either being met or are not. Disruption or strengthening of the relationship might occur, even in long-married couples.

Bernard Murstein proposed another theory that suggested three phases of relationship development.[4] Initial attraction, according to Murstein, is usually based on similarities (stimulus variables). As the relationship deepens, partners compare values, looking first to determine if both have the same general

**A Traditional Conceptualization
of the Path to Marriage**

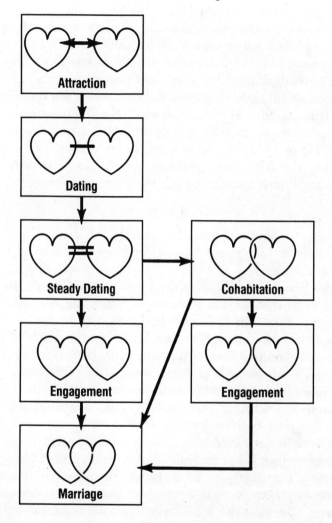

Figure 2-1

values (e.g., if both are Christian) and then looking at more specific values (e.g., the importance of the authority of Scripture). If the relationship is still promising, couples examine the roles they play with each other; that is, how do they act in each other's presence?

Differences in personality and culture can affect the relative importance of the stages in a relationship. Some people, like James and Caroline, introduced at the beginning of the chapter, simply have little interest in discussing values or roles. However, within middle socioeconomic status couples and with professional couples, value consensus is usually the most important aspect of relationships. Because most pastors, psychologists, and other people involved in premarital counseling are professionals (e.g., from middle SES occupations), they will probably construct premarital counseling programs that stress consensus of values. However, their clientele might be of lower SES and thus not share the counselor's feelings about value consensus. The professional must remain sensitive to his or her clients.

LOVE

Almost no one can describe exactly what love is. But we can usually tell when we have it, and we certainly hurt when we lose it.

Aside from cynical definitions—such as George Bernard Shaw's view that love is a game exaggerating the difference between one person and everybody else, or H. L. Mencken's tongue-in-cheek observation that love is the triumph of imagination over intelligence—Murstein probably offers as good a definition as anyone. He defines love as *"a decision on the part of an individual in regard to another person as a love object, the conditions for defining love varying from individual to individual."* [5] He thus defines love as an individual act of the will, subjectively determined.

However, love is too multifaceted to be described in a single definition. For example, C. S. Lewis described four kinds of love, basing them on four Greek words: *agape, storge, phyllia,* and *eros.* [6] Because the Bible says that God is *agape* and it admonishes people to agape one another, we know that unselfish, giving love is a worthy goal for humans to aim for. But we know, too, that Scripture recognizes other types of love.

In describing a marriage relationship, several theorists have made useful distinctions about how love changes as it grows. Murstein identifies three types of love: passionate, companionate, and romantic love. [7] Passionate love is intense absorption in another involving physiological arousal and attributions of desire and attraction. Companionate love is a strong bond that includes tender attachment, enjoyment of the other's company, and friendship. Romantic love is a combination of passionate and companionate loves, involving acceptance, affection, and commitment.

Passionate love is sustained by lack of consummation early in the relationship. When lovers become a couple, the fires of passion wane, becoming either quenched or banked, ready to flame afresh if fanned by a new stimulus such as reconciliation after conflict, reunion after separation, or experience of an emotion-arousing event together. Companionate love generally increases continually with time. Romantic love varies in parallel with marital satisfaction, decreasing as childrearing and career duties increase, then increasing again in later years as the career winds down and the children leave home.

Robert Sternberg proposed a somewhat different understanding of love.[8] He conceptualized love as consisting of passion, intimacy, and decision/commitment. In the stage of attraction, passion predominates. Intimacy grows as the partners share time and activities. At some point, each partner might commit to continuing the relationship, either deliberately or through default.

In designating a premarital counseling program, the counselor must avoid idealizing any type of love. Rather, the counselor must help the partners assess their emphases and learn to use their ideals of a good marriage to appreciate their strengths and not dwell on their weaknesses.

HOW COMMITMENT DEVELOPS

Whatever love is, the love belonging to marriage involves commitment. Commitment is an act of the will. The person decides simply to be committed and maintains that commitment through thick and thin. Such unwavering fidelity is easier for some people than others by virtue of their upbringing and their personality. Clearly, in the Christian walk with God, such unwavering fidelity is expected. God hates divorce (Mal. 2:16).

Yet, when the partners begin premarital counseling, they have not yet taken the wedding vows. Their commitment is not yet a covenant before God. How do they get to the point of commitment? One helpful way to think about commitment was proposed by Rusbult, who defined commitment by an equation.[9]

Commitment = Satisfactions + Investments − Alternatives

The beginning of a relationship is usually fueled by passion. Relationship satisfaction is high at that point. If the alternatives to the new relationship are undesirable—such as being lonely or going out with an unattractive person—then the satisfactions with the new relationship outweigh the alternatives and the relationship will grow. The closer the partners come to marriage, the more they invest in the relationship, and the more committed they become.

HOW RELATIONSHIPS END

Between 35 and 45 percent of all engagements break up.[10] Sometimes it seems to us as counselors that breakup is inevitable, or that it might be better if a couple did break up. Research has shown that breakup can often be predicted.

Hill, Rubin, and Peplau surveyed 231 men and women who were steadily dating.[11] After 2 years, 103 couples had broken up. Generally, most individuals said that they just lost interest in the relationship. When couples who broke up were compared with the ones who continued to date, they did not differ according to whether they were having sexual intercourse or were cohabiting. Only slight differences were found for similarity of age, educational achievement, educational plans, and physical attractiveness, with the couples who continued to date being slightly more similar than those who broke up. The largest differences between the two groups were that the continuing daters had dated longer and more frequently than those who broke up, and they expressed more closeness, more love, and more intention to marry than those who broke up.

Breaking up is usually not a joint decision. In Hill, Rubin, and Peplau's longitudinal study, about 85 percent of the couples described the decision to break up as due to one person rather than to both people.[12] However, in about half of the cases, each said that he or she had initiated the breakup rather than the partner. Overall, regardless of who initiated the breakup, women usually experienced more sadness, depression, loneliness, and anger than did men.

CONSIDERATIONS FOR DESIGNING PREMARITAL COUNSELING PROGRAMS

By the time different engaged couples are ready for premarital counseling, they have gotten to different positions at different speeds by different paths. This suggests two points. First, *some relationship history is appropriate* when counseling an individual couple or when counseling small groups of couples. Some structured measures of relationships are available.[13] Second, *some assessment is needed.* The premarital counselor needs to be aware of the types of couples attending the program so that he or she can adjust the presentation or exercises to fit the couples. Assessment can be formal or informal.

Some counselors assess the personalities of the potential partners, assuming that partners who have compatible personalities will make compatible spouses. They give couples instruments such as the Myers-Briggs Type Indicator[14] or the Taylor-Johnson Temperament Survey.[15] These instruments might be useful in premarital counseling because (1) couples usually enjoy learning about their personalities; (2) despite the risk that large discrepancies in scores might be given too much importance by the couples (and sometimes the counselor), large discrepancies are of some concern and should be discussed by the partners; and (3) the inventories usually stimulate conversation.

Premarital counseling programs can teach couples to remain sensitive to variations in commitment. The partners can be taught that if they determine that their commitment is waning, they can initiate changes by affecting any of the three parts of the commitment: satisfactions, investments, or alternatives.

In premarital counseling, *counselors can help the couple spot the signs of a relationship breakup.* Fading commitment can be signaled by lowered relationship satisfaction, such as brooding over problems in the relationship, focusing on unsatisfying aspects of the relationship, or lowered investment in the relationship.

Because many troubled relationships do not end prior to marriage, *counselors often need to make additional counseling available to the premarital couples.* That additional counseling might be individual counseling for one partner (if breakup should occur) or postmarital counseling (if the couple has trouble adjusting to marriage). Finally, even if the couple successfully adjusts to marriage, a positive experience with premarital counseling might help the spouses be receptive to marital enrichment programs later in their marriage.

Finally, *although relationships develop in predictable ways, there are many variations from the norm.* Those exceptions make it imperative that our premarital counseling programs allow for individual differences within moral boundaries.

Now that we have reviewed the forces that bring a couple to marriage, our next two chapters will look briefly at the forces that shape that marriage once it has occurred: theology, sociology, and psychology.

CHAPTER THREE

FORCES THAT SHAPE
MODERN MARRIAGES

FOR BETTER OR FOR WORSE, marriage has changed in the twentieth century. To design effective counseling, professionals must understand the factors that have led to some of these changes. This chapter will look at two of them: theology and sociology.

A THEOLOGY OF MARRIAGE

Most pastors and even mental health workers who are Christians have several basic needs in employing a program of preparation for marriage. One of the first is a solid understanding of the theology of marriage upon which to build.

Marriage exists within a context that includes (1) God's eternal truths about the mystery of marriage, (2) society's shared understanding of marriage, including the way we interpret God's truths about marriage, and (3) each married partner's psychological makeup in which his or her understanding of God's and society's image of marriage is acted out.

Each part of this context is interdependent. God's truths are eternal, but we each interpret those truths in light of our society and our personalities. We also must interpret those truths as responsibly as we can in light of historic Christianity. God will empower us through the Holy Spirit to act out those truths and will correct our theology if we are open to the correction.

Note that this discussion focuses on *a* theology of marriage. Only God knows *the* theology of marriage. My understanding might differ from that of some. In my understanding of God's design for marriage, I will consider singleness and chastity, family and adulthood, marrying, and living in marriage.

Singleness and Chastity

God created marriage. People didn't. In the beginning, God surveyed Adam, his handiwork, and said, "It is not good that the man should be alone" (Gen. 2:18). God is sufficient to meet all of our needs. Through interaction with each part of the Trinity, we can have an intimate and effective life. However, God in his wisdom provided other people to *enrich* our meaning and to be vehicles through which he meets our needs, and we meet theirs.

God calls people into different paths of meaningfulness (1 Cor. 7:8–9, 17, 25–40). Some people he calls to marriage. In those instances, married couples can stand as a beacon to the world, showing in the close personal relationship of marriage what an intimate relationship can consist of, and thereby helping others understand what a close relationship with God can consist of.

However, God did not call all people into marriage. Those who are not married are as valuable as the married and can live lives that are fully as rich as the married. The single person can experience intimacy with God, family of origin, extended family, other Christians, and non-Christians.

People called to singleness are also called to sexual chastity— whether heterosexual or homosexual. God calls the unmarried to refrain from sexual intercourse. In 1 Corinthians 6:15–20, Paul argues that the sexual joining of a man and woman outside of the covenant of marriage is like the joining of a person's spirit to a god who is not God. He thus calls us to shun such immorality.

Family and Adulthood

The history of Christianity is the history of a family. It began with the creative act of God in the Garden of Eden and continued even with the rebellion of God's created people.

Jesus taught the meaning of the family of God. When his mother and brothers came to Jesus while he was teaching, he asked, "Who are my mother and brothers? . . . Whoever does the will of God is my brother, and sister, and mother" (Mark 3:31–35). Thus, Jesus taught that the true family of God was the family of the covenant rather than the family of birth. This does not allow people to be irresponsible to their families of origin. Even Jesus on the cross made provision for his mother's well-being (John 19:26–27). Further, we are admonished by Paul to care for our families (1 Tim. 5:8).

Families are clearly charged with the responsibility for the spiritual maturity of the children within the family (see Deut. 6:7). By our words and lives, we either teach children that God is indispensable to life or that he is simply just another set of values.

The child enters adolescence and adulthood with family-conditioned beliefs and values about God and his place in the life of the individual, the marriage, and the family. Many of those beliefs have been learned not through verbal teaching or our own personal experience but through observation of our families. Because the beliefs have been learned nonverbally, they are often acted out without thinking about why we believe as we do.

Marrying

Every permanent relationship in God's kingdom—including marriage—is built on covenant. In the covenant of marriage, sacrifice and death are required: Marriage within the church identifies the couple with the death of Jesus. In so doing, the spouses pledge to die to self and to live for the partner. Each says, in effect, "Through the power of God's Holy Spirit, I attach myself to Jesus who will help me to die to my own desires, putting your, my beloved's, desires and needs above my own." Marriage is based on mutual self-sacrifice.

The covenant ceremony of marriage, in which mutual self-sacrifice is pledged, is followed by giving one's own body to the other in sexual intercourse. Paul captures this eloquently, "For the wife does not rule over her own body, but the husband does; likewise the husband does not rule over his own body, but the wife does" (1 Cor. 7:4).

Living in Marriage

The goal of a covenant is knowledge of the other person—total knowledge in spirit, soul, and body. Genesis 4:1 says, "Now Adam knew Eve his wife, and she conceived and bore Cain. . . ." God's provision for complete knowledge of another person is the covenant. Derek Prince describes how two words are used for sexual intercourse throughout the Bible.[1] If the sexual intercourse is within the covenant of marriage, the Bible says that a man *knows* his wife. If the sexual contact is outside of the covenant of marriage, the Bible says that a man *lies with* a woman. It is through covenant that real knowledge of one's partner is obtained.

The principles of living in marriage are the principles of covenant living: mutual self-sacrifice or agape love. Paul argues in Ephesians 5 to "Be subject to one another out of reverence for Christ" (v. 21). In the following verses, he illustrates this principle of mutual self-sacrifice by several examples. He tells husbands and wives that regardless of the roles they are in, they are to care more about the welfare of the spouse than about themselves. He tells children to meet their parents' needs for honor and respect, and he tells parents to meet the needs of their children for discipline and instruction, and an absence of provocation to anger. He tells slaves to serve their masters with diligence and sincerity, and he tells masters to treat their slaves kindly and impartially. I don't believe that the passage from Ephesians 5:21 to 6:9 is a prescription for God-ordained roles in marriage, family, and master-slave relations. Rather, the passage teaches that whatever roles we are in, whether we like them or not, whether we think they are equitable or not, we are to be self-sacrificial in our love. And we are to place the needs of others over our own.

Living within a marriage is based on the foundation that we are children of a covenant with God and are to let love be our aim, placing others' good before our own in an atmosphere of mutual self-sacrifice, which knits us together with God into a threefold cord. And remember: "A threefold cord is not quickly broken" (Eccles. 4:12b).

A SOCIOLOGY OF MARRIAGE

Besides a theological understanding of marriage, we also need to grasp a *sociology* of marriage, which sets it in societal context and shows the place of the church within that society. My goal in this section is to analyze the social forces operating during the last quarter of the twentieth century as they affect marriages. I hope that such an analysis will help us understand the environment into which newlyweds are entering. In general, it is a world that is hostile to marriage as Christians have traditionally understood it. For our purposes, I offer three classes of social forces: technical innovations, social trends, and philosophical trends.

Technical Innovations

Improved health care has led to an increased average life span: for adults now, it's about seventy-five years for men, and eighty-three years for women—instead of about fifty as it was at the end of the nineteenth century.

With the increasing life *span* has come a radical shift in the nature of the life *cycle.* [2] Imagine the adult of 1900. He or she probably was raised in a family until reaching adolescence. At age fifteen to eighteen, the person married and began to raise his or her own family—often including five to fifteen children. About three years after the last child left home, the adult could expect death (probably due to exhaustion). The entire life span was involved in either being in or rearing a family. So the family was of supreme importance.

Contrast that with the modern adult. The adult lives within the family for about eighteen years, then he or she leaves for college or work. But the typical adult does not marry until about age twenty-three for females and twenty-five for males. The couple may have one, two, or (with increasing frequency) no children. Childrearing will occupy about twenty years at the most, before the children leave home. After that, the couple can expect about thirty years before death. Only about half of the life span is involved in family concerns instead of essentially the entire life as it did in 1900. Thus, the impact of improved health care has affected people's value on the family.

Technological advances in birth control have also affected preparation for marriage. Since the 1960s, new birth control technologies have increased the attention we pay to sex, because people now can engage in sexual intercourse without apparent serious repercussions. Thus, the level of premarital sexual experience is high. About half of the women and over half of the men have had sexual experience by the age of nineteen.[3]

There is evidence that the rate of sexual experience is high even among people reared in conservative religious homes.[4] This suggests that the premarital counselor can no longer pitch his or her discussions of sex at the uninformed virgin. On the other hand, the counselor cannot assume that every couple is sexually sophisticated, either. Rather, the wise counselor might divide couples into those with high and low degrees of sexual experience and counsel each differently.

In addition, the new birth control technologies have led to a dramatic increase in nonmarital cohabitation.[5] According to statistics from the U.S. Bureau of the Census, between 1970 and 1984 the rate of cohabitation quadrupled, increasing substantially even among Christians. These couples are not naive about sex nor about the problems of daily living. Counselors who do not recognize the experiences of cohabiting couples risk alienating them from any future counsel because the couples label the counselor's help as irrelevant.

Another technological revolution was begun by the microchip. Naisbitt has ably described some of the implications of this revolution.[6] One effect is that we are no longer a world driven by industrial output. We are a world driven by information.

For the premarital counselor, this means that couples are information rich. I recently talked to an articulate man who had gone through a rather extensive premarital counseling program at his church. He said that he liked the program and recommended it for anyone. When I asked him what he had learned from the counseling, he said thoughtfully, "I don't think I learned a single thing that I didn't already know. The pastor just put it together nicely."

The premarital counselor must change his or her goals to accommodate these increasingly sophisticated couples. Instead of aiming at teaching what couples do not know, the counselor might strive to place the information in a form that is easily used by the couple.

Social Trends

The industrial revolution, in which a mass migration from rural to urban areas occurred in the late nineteenth century, uprooted the family from its usual family-of-origin context and isolated nuclear families from wider familial support networks. Further, even the marriage has been increasingly threatened as adult workers have been thrown into daily contact with adults of the other sex in modern society as opposed to the agrarian community in which men usually worked with men and women with women. Industrialization thus weakened both the extended family and the marriage.

Another important trend has been the women's movement. Many Christians may be hostile to the methods and even some of the aims of the radical members of the women's movement; but few can deny that it has generated major positive effects (and some that might not be considered so positive).

Because of the women's movement, our view of sex roles has changed. Traditional sex roles have all but been abandoned in many parts of society. While many women still elect to stay home with their children (which I think is great), stereotypes such as "washing dishes is women's work" or "a man's work is to lift heavy objects and spit in the dirt" are rarely endorsed today. Each couple must now negotiate its own "rules."

Rachel Hare-Mustin has argued that the biggest effect of the women's movement is that more women have entered the labor force.[7] There are several results of this. First, many couples depend on two incomes to maintain a high standard of living, and they continue to want two incomes, even after children are born. Second, many women derive benefits to their self-esteem from their employment, which results in less dependency on the spouse for self-esteem. Third, women and men each face a myriad of time demands from work. Less time is left for each other. Fourth, men and women are increasingly working on equal levels, which increases the number and strength of sexual attractions that must be dealt with by spouses in the work place. Fifth, the variety of family forms has increased relative to past years.[8]

On the other hand, some women have tired of trying to work full time outside the home, be a mother and wife, have friends, and occasionally get a chance to sit down. Many mothers have thus decided to give up some of the conveniences and even luxuries of the two-income family for more time with children and husband. Further, there is increasing concern over latchkey children and disease within institutional day-care settings. Only time will tell which trend will predominate. The premarital counselor must take the social climate into account and prepare couples to deal with the pressures they will encounter in modern society.

Partly because of the women's movement and the increasing normalcy of the two-earner household and partly for other reasons, the standard of living experienced by most United States citizens—including the average couple attending premarital counseling—is extremely high.

This high standard of living brings with it four modern attitudes: affluence, easy credit, disposability, and the pursuit of pleasure. Affluence feeds upon itself. We become addicted to *things*: two cars, video recorders, stylish clothes, fancy food, eating out, maid service, and electric gadgets and appliances. This may lead to the danger of overspending due to easy credit. Many couples need help with budgeting and living within their means, whether they are from high- or low-income families. Related to affluence is a sense of disposability. If we tire of something, we get rid of it. Is something too much trouble? Throw it away. And related to both affluence and disposability is the pursuit of pleasure. We continually look for things that make us feel good. Having money to buy whatever we wish (and liberal credit), we indulge our passions.

The consequences of these attitudes can show up in the way

we think about marriage relationships; marriage can become just another "thing." We do not automatically dispose of it if problems arise, but we may think of ourselves as being *able* to dispose of it if the marriage causes too much discomfort or costs too much. Marriages are evaluated in terms of the pleasure they bring.

The implication of this for the premarital counselor is that notions of commitment, permanence in relationship, and marriage as a covenant are foreign to most couples raised outside of the church—and to many couples raised inside the church. The counselor must exert special effort to educate the couple about Christian marriage as covenant, and be prepared for a high rate of rejection of those ideas.

Philosophical Trends

Schaeffer has suggested that the philosophical climate of modern times is due largely to Hegel's concept of the dialectic, a *process* of reasoning.[9] The dialectic acknowledged the existence of theses and their opposites (antitheses), but it said that the real truth was in the form of some compromise (or synthesis) between the two extremes. However, once this synthesis was stated, it became a statement of fact, a thesis. It in turn had its antithesis. The new thesis and antithesis could also be synthesized. By outlining this dialectical process of forming ever-newer syntheses from opposites, Hegel thus created a new understanding that the only absolute truth was the dialectical process, itself.

In the twentieth century, Hegel's influence is widespread. We rarely look for truth in terms of *facts* anymore. We describe truth in terms of *processes*. The main effect of process reasoning for the premarital counselor involves the viewpoints of the couples who will be counseled. Many have lost a sense of Scripture as an absolutely true authority. What's worse, they may not even realize that they devalue God's word.

On a more global level, many have lost the belief in causal reasoning. We frequently hear the statement that no one is responsible for marriage troubles, meaning no one is *totally* responsible for marriage troubles. Each is responsible for his or her own behavior.

27

Another philosophical trend affecting premarital counseling is the always tenuous balance between communal responsibility and individual liberty. The balance is reflected in our two political parties, and in the system of checks and balances in government, the framing of the Constitution, and in countless other ways.

In recent years, the pendulum appears to have swung toward more emphasis on individual liberty than on communal responsibility. In marriages, this has shown up as an emphasis on rights, to the exclusion of responsibilities, and on contracts, to the exclusion of covenants. Bromley and Busching, who recently contrasted contracts and covenants,[10] argue essentially that a contract says, "I'll do my part and you do yours. If we're lucky everything will work out for both of us." A covenant, on the other hand, says, "I'll give you 100 percent forever, even if you never give me anything back, because I love you."

The general societal shift from a covenantal to contractual perspective has several implications. A contract mentality means that couples often make premarital agreements that specify the rights of each spouse and may even prescribe the division of property should the marriage end in divorce.

Further, lawsuits have become prominent. This has occurred within marriages and families, with divorce and child custody litigation being frequent. Unhappily, the premarital counselor might someday expect to be sued by the divorcing couple who believed that he or she promised a happy marriage.

The United States was founded on the principle of majority rule with respect for the rights of the minority. In recent years, we have departed from that standard to a concept of rule so that no minority is offended. This stance has made most minorities happier, but has eroded the ability of the nation to take a positive value stance.

One consequence of this is that we have lost a vision for what a marriage or family should be like. We have moved to the concept that "marriages" and "families" imply *many* ideal types of marriages and families. People are reluctant to endorse any one ideal for marriage because they can always think of a minority group of people who do not fit the ideal. The Bergers[11] argue persuasively that diversity in types of existing marriages does not imply that there *should* be diverse types of marriage.

For the premarital counselor, the implications are that one should not be afraid to propose ideals for a good marriage, including those proposed by Scripture. Our inability consistently to live up to an ideal should not prevent us from adopting that ideal as a goal.

Our response to these changes in technological, social, and philosophical trends can be varied. We may lament the changes or applaud them. But regardless, we must deal with them if we are to counsel effectively. As Christians, we also must stand for righteousness and biblical Christianity in our counseling; but we must do so in ways that can be understood by the twentieth- and twenty-first-century Christian.

CHAPTER FOUR

A PSYCHOLOGY OF MARRIAGE

HAVING BEEN AN ENGINEER WHEN I WAS YOUNGER, I sometimes think in rather concrete images. For example, I can easily conceptualize a man and woman about to marry as if they were placing two gear wheels close to each other. Each gear wheel has an assortment of teeth and grooves. What will happen when the two gear wheels actually come together? That depends on four things: communication (the interplay between the gears), the closeness of the fit, the struggle between the two gears, and the degree to which the gears stay in contact through the heat of conflict.

Premarriage counselors need an understanding of the psychology of love and marriage that places marriage within the theological and societal context. This "gear model" illustrates four important psychological aspects of marriage involved throughout the entire family life cycle.[1] Further, it suggests that marriage involves change, which both partners must deal with.

COMMUNICATION

Any communication can be understood in terms of its semantics, its syntax, or its pragmatics.[2]

The *semantics* of communication is the meaning of what is expressed. A counselor who emphasizes semantics makes sure each spouse fully understands what the other spouse means and reminds couples that problems occur because people do not understand each other's meaning. The solution to problems logically follows: If people can be helped to communicate accurately and empathically, then problems will disappear.

The *syntax* of communication is how communications are punctuated. The punctuation marks of conversations are emotions. Counselors who emphasize the syntax of communications will pay particular attention to the emotional expression of each partner. Such counselors assume that problems occur because people say things in unproductive ways. The obvious solution, then, is for the counselor to help the couple change the ways they are talking and arguing.

The *pragmatics* of communication involves the practical effects of a communication.[3] For instance, a communication could produce the desired effect—or an unanticipated and undesired effect. Usually, when unanticipated effects of communication occur, it is because one of the spouses' "rules" of communication has been violated. A "rule" is simply an experience-based expectation about how communications proceed. Problems are assumed to be not so much due to *what* is said or *how* it is said as to the *effects* of the communication on the partner. Problems can be solved, then, by changing communications so they produce the desired effects.

Importantly, the semantics, syntax, or pragmatics of communication occur simultaneously. A counselor must emphasize one of the three. There is not enough time to focus on all three parts of communication, and trying to do so often confuses the couple about what is being emphasized.

Poor communication—whether it is misunderstanding each other's meanings, punctuating communications in harmful ways, or communicating in ways that don't achieve desired effects—is a ticket to marriage problems. Thus, the premarital couple must develop patterns of communication that will satisfy them, allow them to remain in intellectual and emotional contact, and grow together throughout their marriage.

CLOSENESS

There are different types of intimacy.[4] *Emotional intimacy* includes feeling close to each other and feeling that the spouse is supportive during times of emotional upheaval and stress. *Sexual intimacy* includes feeling that the sexual act is more than a physical release. *Social intimacy* involves having social activities in common, such as attending social events at church or with one partner's colleagues at work or spending time with families of origin. *Recreational intimacy* involves the pleasurable use of leisure time together. *Intellectual intimacy* involves the enjoyment each partner experiences in sharing ideas.

Each of the five types of intimacy is not equally important to all couples. People use each day's activities to regulate their needs for various intimate time, time alone, and non-intimate time with others. When their intimacy is unbalanced, they will be unhappy and will try to adjust the activities of their typical day to re-balance their intimacy. Problems can arise in marriage when spouses differ in levels of desired intimacy, distance, or coaction, and expect that their spouse alone will meet all of their needs. Thus, in premarital counseling, the counselor must help couples see that the spouse is not totally responsible for meeting all of the intimacy needs of the partner. The partners are shown ways each can satisfy his or her needs for intimacy while not threatening the spouse. The only exception is sexual intimacy, which makes it important for the premarital counselor to deal explicitly with the sexual relationship between the couple, for no one but the spouse should meet that need.

CONFLICT

Conflict happens even in the best marriages. Premarital couples must learn how to deal with conflict productively. I emphasize the pragmatics of communication, so my focus in conflict resolution is on the effects communications have on the partner. I may show a couple that the *intent* of the communication was not the same as the *impact* on the spouse.

Further, I may have couples read Fisher and Ury's *Getting to Yes*,[5] an excellent book on negotiating differences of opinion. The authors suggest that people become locked into power struggles because they declare their positions and try to persuade and coerce their partners to accept those positions. The authors observe that people's *interests* are really more fundamental than the position they take. They have found that both sides' interests usually may be satisfied with a creative solution—if each side can put aside the position it originally declared and can try to *create* ways that meet the interests of both parties. I have found Fisher and Ury's method to be extremely effective, and so have most of my clients.

I teach each partner to recognize when a power struggle is beginning—usually recognizable because the person mentally rehearses a dialogue with the other person. (*Who does he think he is? He doesn't have the right to say that to me. I can't stand it when he is so bossy.*)

Once both partners can recognize the beginning of a power struggle, they can interrupt their internal dialogue and plan ways to calm themselves, perhaps by thinking instructions to themselves such as, *calm down. Don't get into a tizzy over something so minor.* Once calm, each partner considers how important the issue seems to himself or herself and how important the issue seems to his or her partner, usually through talking with the partner. They should then remind themselves of the marriage covenant, that each person is responsible for submitting to the other.

The man particularly should be willing to take the lead in giving up his selfish desires for the good of his wife, because in my view, spiritual leadership has much less to do with leading home devotions than it does with initiating reconciliation after disagreement, showing love for the spouse, and forgiving her when she has hurt her husband. Being an example of Christ's love is a more powerful way to lead than by lecturing or teaching about it.

Unfortunately, we live after the Fall. Thus, there are times when a covenant mentality and spiritual leadership by the husband will not result in resolving the conflict. At those times, rather than get into a cycle of blame and recrimination between spouses, the couple must accept that they are imperfect and employ Fisher and Ury's problem-solving strategy to identify their own interests (in writing if possible) and then to create some heretofore unthought-of solution that meets most of each person's interests.

COMMITMENT

Marriage depends on commitment, which in turn depends on satisfaction and investments. Of course, commitment may be reduced if a person is attracted to a competing relationship. One theory suggests that satisfaction, and thus commitment, depends on each partner's perception of the fairness of, or equity in, the relationship. Equity occurs when the perceived balance of rewards received and investments made by each spouse is about the same. For example, a husband might gain many rewards but also have many investments in a marriage. He might be just as satisfied with the relationship as his wife, who has few rewards but also few investments. A perceived imbalance in such rewards and investments would make for an inequitable marriage in the mind of at least one of the spouses.

Another theory proposes that satisfaction depends on feeling that the relationship is rewarding. Cate, Lloyd, and Long compared these two theories with ninety individuals involved in premarital relationships of different degrees of seriousness from casual dating to engagement.[6] Using questionnaires, they tested the participants at two times, three months apart. They found that the level of perceived rewards was a better predictor of involvement with the relationship than were perceptions of equity of rewards and investments.

As with most secular theories, the researchers assumed that people evaluate their relationship exclusively in terms of what they get out of it. With a covenant-based marriage, the perception of fairness or equality of rewards should be expected to be less important than suggested by secular theories of social exchange. In addition, a Christian considers his or her spouse and reminds himself or herself of the covenant commitment they share. These thoughts might cement commitment to the marriage—even when the going is extremely rough.

COPING WITH CHANGES

The paradox of marriage is that people desire to create stable, permanent, fulfilling relationships that involve communication, closeness, conflict management, and commitment; yet stability can only be found amidst continued change. People are continually changing—in response to their own internal lives, in response to partners' behaviors, in response to things that happen to them in environments outside the marriage, and in response to the direct intervention of God. Changes may be superficial or substantial, significant or insignificant, precipitous or slowly evolving. People may change their thought, behaviors, and emotions. They may change cognitively, morally, spiritually, bodily, and psychologically. Some changes are also due to decisions, such as to change jobs, return to college, or retire. Change is as necessary to a good marriage as is stability. Both changes and efforts to cope with those changes affect marriage relationships.

Changes Before Marriage

Lewis has described six stages that premarital relationships pass through: perceiving similarities, achieving pair rapport, engaging in mutual self-disclosure, role taking, developing interpersonal role fit, and reaching crystallization as a couple.[7] In the first three stages, the couple usually becomes increasingly closer. The perception of similarities (stage 1) enhances a feeling of intimacy at a basic level. Pair rapport (stage 2) and self-disclosure (stage 3) usually focus on communication. With role taking and achieving interpersonal role fit (stages 4 and 5), the couple communicates and grows in intimacy but mostly they learn to resolve conflicts and differences. At the final stage, crystallization, the couple builds commitment to each other as they undertake activities that make them identify themselves as a couple and that cause other people—family, friends, and perhaps coworkers—to identify them as a couple. During each of the changes to a different stage, the couple can either adjust to the change, or fail to cope with it in a way that is good for their relationship.

Changes at the Transition to Marriage

After the wedding, the couple must adjust to living together in marriage. With this adjustment comes the potential that their patterns of intimacy, distance, and coaction will be seriously disrupted. Because they are spending more time together and much of it is a different type of time, couples often change their perceptions about their closeness.

Some of the changes might be dramatic. For example, the couple will likely have a richer sexual relationship than they had prior to marriage. They will also have new opportunities and new topics about which to communicate. However, their communication patterns are likely to be disrupted by conflict, not only because they must resolve potentially controversial topics, such as finances and in-laws, but also because they are likely to spend more time together and have different ideas about how to use that time. Thus, the transition to marriage affords opportunities to use their general communication, conflict management, and problem-solving skills.

Changes During the First Three Years of Marriage

Most divorces occur within the first three years of marriage.[8] Usually, the first year involves two phases: a honeymoon period in which little disagreement occurs, and later, a period when the spouses begin to assert their own ideas rather than to automatically accede to their partner's wishes. This ushers in a period of conflict and negotiation that may be necessary to the formation of a stable happy marriage. When couples do not work out their differences within the first three years, they may harbor resentment, which may grow into large disagreements.

In the second year of marriage, untroubled couples often enjoy stability in their relationships, while troubled couples escalate in their conflict and resentment. The third year can be a year of calm for couples who worked out their basic differences during the first year, or it can be a year of acrimony and divorce for couples who could never resolve their differences.

OVERVIEW OF THE
PSYCHOLOGY OF MARRIAGE

Overall, the premarital and early marital periods are crucial in establishing the relationship patterns that will be used throughout much of the partners' remaining married life together. But relationships, like individuals, do not remain static. They are continually changing.

Each of the four primary aspects of relationships—communication, closeness, conflict, and commitment—can be affected by changes in life. The couple must cope with those changes, effectively or ineffectively.

Counseling for troubled marriages usually addresses changes in these four primary aspects. Premarital counseling should, too, because the early stages of the relationship often strongly affect later behavior of the couple. So the partners need to be helped to learn skills necessary to deal with the inevitable changes throughout at least the early part of marriage.

CHAPTER FIVE

CAN CHRISTIANS ACCEPT DIVORCED PEOPLE?

JUST AS IT'S HELPFUL FOR A PREMARRIAGE COUNSELOR to understand a theology of marriage, as described in chapter 3, it's also important for counselors who will be dealing with remarrying couples to understand divorce. In this chapter, I will first outline four fundamental positions regarding divorce and then describe some of the assumptions of each position. For this discussion, I will draw heavily from an analysis of C. J. Barber, who reviewed thirty-one books by Christian authors on marriage, divorce, and remarriage.[1] Then I will outline several cases and describe the position I think is theologically appropriate in each.

FOUR FUNDAMENTAL POSITIONS ON DIVORCE

Marriage Is Permanent—Period

The fundamental belief advocated by Laney[2] is that marriage was created and ordained by God and that only God can end marriage. By this Laney suggests that death is the only legitimate means of ending a marriage (Mark 10:6–9). He argues that marriage among Christians is permanent—no exceptions—and discounts two potential exceptions mentioned in other Gospel accounts. For example, in Matthew's Gospel, Laney argues that Jesus was speaking to Jews, not Christians.

Ideally, Marriage Is Permanent—Except for Adultery

All conservative, evangelical writers agree that God intended marriage to be permanent and that God hates divorce (Mal. 2:16). The fundamental difference between Laney and the others involves the understanding of whether God has established marriage as ideally permanent, but has provided for the human weakness of people falling short of the ideal. Once this belief is accepted, then questions arise as to what can legitimately end a marriage.

One position is that the only exception for ending a marriage of two Christians is adultery (Matt. 5:32 and 19:9).[3] Before Jesus, the penalty for adultery among Jews was death; however, the Romans made it illegal for Jews to inflict the death penalty, so divorce became the substitute, signifying that the marriage relationship was dead. Marriage is to be ended in divorce only as a last resort, with reconciliation always being preferable to divorce. Homosexual adultery also is considered to be grounds for divorce.

A marriage between a Christian and non-Christian operates by other rules. Paul admonished the Christian to be lovingly committed to the non-Christian mate as long as the non-Christian desires. However, if the non-Christian wants to divorce and deserts the Christian, then divorce is permitted (1 Cor. 7:15), though even then reconciliation is preferred.

Ideally Marriage Is Permanent—Except for Exceptional Circumstances

Usually, the exceptional circumstances that might occasion divorce—besides unrepentant adultery, desertion by an unbeliever, or divorce prior to conversion to Christianity—hinge on the interpretation of "hardness of heart." Jesus said that Moses allowed divorce because of the hardness of the hearts of the Israelites (Mark 10:4, 5). Circumstances qualifying as contemporary hardness of heart might include (a) spouse or child abuse, (b) unrepentant and chronic alcoholism or drug addiction, (c) failure to care for one's family (1 Tim. 5:8), which is tantamount to becoming an unbeliever, and (d) refusal to allow the spouse or children to worship God. Increasing numbers of Christians argue that inflicting "mental cruelty" on a spouse or other instances of psychological harm or neglect may be legitimate incidents involving "hardness of heart."

Jesus did not use *moicheia,* the narrower word for adultery, to limit the exceptions to sexual relations while married. Rather, he used *porneia,* which is considerably broader in scope. Ellisen's view suggests that *porneia* might include adultery, unfaithfulness during betrothal, marriage to an unbeliever, or all extramarital sexual relations (e.g., bestiality, homosexuality, incest).[4]

Ideally, Marriage Is Permanent—Except When Annulled by a Church Tribunal

Generally, this is the position of the Roman Catholic Church, which provides for church tribunals that will rule on annulment of a marriage that ended in divorce before annulment procedures were instituted. Proponents of this viewpoint have been Kelly, Young, and Zwack.[5] As Barber points out, this is not a popular position among many evangelical Christians because it emphasizes the authority of priests above the authority of Scripture.[6]

SAMPLE CASES

Case 1: Standing up for Biblical Rights

Barry and Jean have been married nine years. Barry has had an affair, which he claims is the only time that he has been unfaithful. Further, he has said that he learned a hard lesson and intends never to repeat that mistake. Jean is extremely angry and hurt. She quotes Scripture (Matt. 5:32 and 19:9) citing that divorce is her right and she says that she intends to stand on her rights. She has contacted a lawyer. How do you counsel Barry and Jean?

I would be inclined to make sure that Barry is repentant for his behavior and sincere in his statement of future fidelity. I would acknowledge the hurt and pain Jean surely feels and the desire that such anger creates to strike back. I would, though, encourage Jean not to act precipitously in pursuing divorce, stating that God was often forgiving of the spiritual adultery of Israel when Israel repented. At some later session, I would probably discuss the modern "rights" mentality and its opposition to the biblical injunction to forgive. Overall, I would try to dissuade Jean from divorce and work with both partners on issues of trust, trustworthiness, and forgiveness.

Case 2: Repeated Infidelity

Franklin and Kristin have been married thirteen years. Kristin has had six (known) affairs during that time. Each time, she has confessed her sin and begged for forgiveness, and each time Franklin has taken her back. Recently, when Kristin's seventh affair came to light, she again broke it off and asked for forgiveness. Franklin says he has forgiven her, but he is clearly furious with her intractable sexual infidelity. This time, despite forgiving her, he says he intends to divorce her. How should you counsel them?

In the case of repeated sexual infidelity, there comes a time when it is apparent that a spouse does not intend to be or cannot be faithful to the marriage. That determination is always a judgment call. In this case, I would be particularly concerned about Kristin's difficulty in handling her sexual temptations and about Franklin's potential for bitterness despite his assurance that he has really forgiven her. In my view, Franklin would be justified in pursuing divorce on the grounds of *porneia*. Further, he would then be free to remarry, should that become an option in the future. If children are involved, other considerations are needed; what is best for them involves clear judgment appropriate to the specific situation.

Case 3: Homosexuality

Forty-five-year-old Maria sat crying in my office. A student in one of my classes, she had recently found out her husband had been involved in frequent homosexual encounters during their eighteen-year marriage. She was afraid of AIDS, disgusted with her husband's behavior, and devastated by her husband's betrayal of herself and her five children. Maria and her husband were regular church attenders and claimed to be Christians. When confronted, her husband said that he probably would continue the homosexual affairs. She asked what she should do.

I agreed with her decision to be tested for the AIDS virus and to refrain from sexual intercourse with her husband until the future of the marriage was decided. In light of her husband's unrepentant attitude, I suspected that divorce would be forthcoming.

Case 4: Physical Abuse

Noreen has a large bruise on the side of her cheek and other bruises on her arms. She tells you that this is not the first time her husband has hurt her while they were disagreeing. She asks for help in dealing with the situation. What is appropriate?

First, Noreen's husband, Jack, is never within God's law when he abuses his wife. He needs help from a therapist to manage his aggression without using violence, and he needs help in his spiritual walk to prevent such sin and to work through to forgiveness for the sin in the past. Until that help is forthcoming, I would usually advise Noreen to separate from her husband. Second, reconciliation is to be sought, and the separation would be temporary, pending successful help for Jack and successful marriage counseling so they can learn to resolve their differences without violence. Third, if Jack remains abusive, Noreen should

remain separated from him; divorce is improper (see 1 Cor.
7:11). On the other hand, if Jack decides to divorce Noreen or if
either combines the separation with unfaithfulness, there are
scriptural grounds for divorce.

Case 5: An Alcoholic Spouse

Ronald and Lee have been married for twenty-five years. Lee
complains that Ronald has been an alcoholic for their entire marriage but that the drunkenness has recently increased. Since
"the kids" have all grown up, Lee sees no reason to continue her
marriage to Ronald. She is embarrassed by his behavior and believes Ronald sometimes gets drunk just to spite her. She sees
his habitual drunkenness as an instance of "mental abuse" and
"functional desertion." She thus views her desire to obtain a
divorce as scripturally sound. She wants to know your opinion.

I am well aware of the enormous difficulties that can occur
when one or both spouses is alcoholic. However, I do not believe
that alcoholism, itself, is grounds for scripturally consistent divorce. I would recommend family counseling and counseling for
alcoholism.

Case 6: Adultery

Bart and Kathleen had been married for two years when Bart
left Kathleen and moved to Atlanta. Two years after the desertion, Kathleen learned that Bart was living with a woman. She
wants to know whether it is scripturally permissible for her to
initiate a divorce.

Generally, desertion accompanied by proof of sexual infidelity
is thought to fall within the guidelines permitting divorce.

Case 7: Desertion

Bonnie and Will were married for seven years when Bonnie
left Will. Although their relationship had been conflictual for
years, there was no indication that Bonnie had been unfaithful.
Both were members of the church and professed Christianity.
When Bonnie moved from the city in which they had lived
for most of their lives, Will tried to find her and even hired a
private investigator to search for her; but she could not be
found. It has now been seven and one-half years since Bonnie

43

left. Will has become increasingly attracted to a woman in his Bible study with whom he shares much in common. They have asked whether it is permissible for Will to initiate divorce proceedings.

For many, the long absence of Bonnie is clear justification that she does not intend to return to the marriage relationship. Often, there is a presumption that she has become involved in a sexual relationship and has been unfaithful to her marriage vows, so divorce is seen as scripturally permissible. However, Will has remained faithful to Bonnie throughout this period and it might not be accurate to assume that Bonnie has been any less faithful. I believe this case is not covered by clear scriptural principles, so I would leave it to the conscience of Will to decide, within his local community of believing Christians, rather than try to justify it based on Scripture. His decision should be based on prayer and a discernment of God's will for him.

Case 8: Divorce Desired by Christian Spouse

Carol and Rod have been married six turbulent years. They disagree over many things, but especially over religion. Carol is a Christian and is very involved in her church. Rod is not religious. He has objected strenuously to the number of times per week Carol is away from home attending church meetings. Carol thinks Rod is being repressive and restricting her religious freedom. She wants a divorce. Rod feels that religion is interfering with their marriage. He does not want a divorce, but he refuses to go to counseling with Carol's pastor. Carol wants to know if divorce is proper.

According to Paul's instructions (1 Cor. 7:11), Carol should stay with Rod and try to reconcile their relationship. Despite his attitudes toward her Christian beliefs, she should view this as a chance to witness positively to Rod by her proper and chaste behavior—perhaps even by cutting back on her involvement in church activities. If Rod refuses to attend counseling with a pastor or a Christian professional, it would probably still be wiser for Carol and Rod to attend secular marriage therapy than to avoid the counseling.

Case 9: Divorce Desired by Non-Christian Spouse

Eric and Mona have been married four years. Recently, they have begun to disagree frequently and emotionally. Eric is not a Christian, but Mona is. Eric has begun to pressure Mona for a divorce. Mona wants to know what she should do.

Mona's main job should be to try to reconcile their marriage through whatever means are possible. Marriage therapy would be desirable. If serious attempts at reconciliation fail, then divorce is scripturally permissible.

SUMMARY

God hates divorce, but has permitted it under certain circumstances. As a marriage counselor, I want to encourage couples to work hard to avoid divorce, and to divorce only as a last resort. But as a counselor who may be asked to prepare couples for remarriage after a divorce, my focus is different. At that point, the divorce is usually a *fait accompli,* and I must assess the divorced persons' attitude toward divorce. Is it one of brokenness and repentance before God, or one of willful self-justification? Often, the letter of the law is even less important (though God's law is always important) than the condition of the person's heart. God is both righteous and loving. As a counselor, my task in each instance is to discern the appropriate emphasis and act to further the kingdom of God.

CHAPTER SIX

EFFECTS OF WIDOWHOOD AND DIVORCE

MARRIAGE IS CHARACTERIZED BY communication, closeness, conflict resolution, and commitment. Loss of a spouse through death or divorce disrupts all of those parts of the surviving spouse's life. Remarriage necessitates reestablishing them, which, after the previous loss, is even harder than it was in the first marriage.

As a backdrop to understanding how partners enter remarriage, in this chapter, I explore the psychological effects of losing a spouse through death or divorce, as well as sociological factors involved with divorce, and the difficulties in adjusting to it.

THE PSYCHOLOGY OF WIDOWHOOD

The Stressfulness of a Loved One's Death

In Holmes and Rahe's well-known study of the stressfulness of common life events, death of a spouse is at the top of the list—the standard against which all other life events are measured.[1] The mere experience of the death of a spouse gives the person one hundred "life change points." Holmes and Rahe determined that if the person accumulated one hundred additional points, he or she was at risk for serious illness or accidents within the next two years. Unfortunately, death of a spouse is not an isolated event, and it is inevitable that the widow or widower will soon accumulate many other related life change points such as loss of income, moving, change in churches, changes in recreation, work or education.

Grief

After the death of a spouse, the widow or widower experiences grief. Children may also experience grief, but depending on their ages, they might not experience it similarly to adults. For adults and older adolescents, grief usually occurs in three stages over a period of about a year, though it can last longer.[2] In the first stage, which lasts about two to four weeks, the survivor experiences numbed shock. Emotions are usually volatile. At times, the survivor believes emotion is appropriate but is unable to express or feel it. At other times, sadness or anger come unbidden, intruding in seemingly emotionless situations and causing tears to flow during normal conversation.

After several weeks, the person feels depressed and unmotivated. There is a strong need cognitively to review the facts of the death and to try to make sense of them. Responsibility is alternately assumed or denied for aspects of the death over which the survivor had little or no control. For example, the wife might wail, "If only I had made him wear his seatbelt. . . ." "If only . . ." is one of the dominant themes of the second stage of grief. Over time, this wife will likely come to terms with her inability to control her husband's life, but in the second period of grief her if-only speculations are usual.

47

Besides the continual cognitive review of the death of the spouse, survivors engage in continual social review. They talk about the death to many people. In fact, they often discuss the death so much that their friends tire of hearing about it. In both cognitive and social review, the person is trying to understand the meaning of the death. He or she will inquire into God's purposes for the death, and may question God or be angry with him during this period. Eventually, the person will establish some meaningful understanding and the questioning will slow or stop. Unfortunately, sometimes the meaning one finds in the event results in lasting anger or bitterness. Usually, though, the person is able to get on with his or her life.

Usually within a year of the death, the person will consciously decide "Well, I miss my spouse and life will never be the same without him (or her), but I must cope with the joys and trials of life without him (or her)." After that, the spouse will recall the death and remember the spouse, but the sense of obsessive cognitive and social review will be gone, and the person generally deals with life psychologically much as he or she did before the death.

Disruptions After Death of a Loved One

Being psychologically able to cope with life as one did prior to the death is not the whole story. The death of a loved one has a number of effects—on communication, closeness, conflict management, and commitment—that changes the survivor's life.

Communication. The family had established a pattern of communication over time. Although the communication might not have been optimal (whose communication is?), it was familiar, and that familiarity gave a sense of stability. When the spouse became ill or was tragically involved in an accident, the patterns of communication were disrupted. If the deceased spouse was greatly involved in usual familial communication, the loss of the spouse will force a large transformation on the family system. Perhaps the deceased spouse was more emotionally supportive of other family members than was the surviving spouse. Then pressure will be exerted on the surviving spouse to provide emotional support, which he or she might not feel capable or willing to provide. Conversely, pressure is exerted on the children and the surviving spouse to find supportive communication from others—friends or relatives.

Closeness. When a spouse dies, the intimacy patterns in the entire family are disrupted. This void in intimacy must be coped with, sometimes leading family members to seek emotional closeness from others not within the family. This is one reason some people remarry soon after the death of a spouse. On the other hand, Hetherington, Stanley-Hagan, and Anderson have found that young girls who lose their fathers by death are often slower to develop heterosexual relationships than girls whose fathers are still alive. In contrast, girls who lose their fathers by divorce are often accelerated in their development of heterosexual relationships relative to girls whose parents are not divorced.[3]

Conflict resolution. Within a family, conflict resolution often follows a pattern.[4] For example, at the onset of adolescence, an early adolescent boy will often gain power within the family at the expense of the mother. The mother generally senses the emerging independence of the adolescent boy before the father does, and she often tries to forestall it. Her communications, even in well-functioning families, change from those she used in the family when the boy was in elementary school. She often gives orders with little explanation about why the orders should be followed. When the son objects, an argument may follow. The father often enters the foray between mother and son attempting to be the peacemaker. Depending on how the father handles the situation he may be more or less successful at helping resolve the conflict. In the first year of early adolescence, a pattern of conflict usually emerges by which the family deals with the son's transition to adolescence. The pattern is different with daughters. Usually, behavior patterns between fathers and daughters are subject to more change than are those between mothers and daughters. In particular, girls usually learn their cross-sex social interactional skills through their relationships with their father. They may have some conflict with their mother, but generally less than adolescent boys have with their mother. Often the mother-daughter relationship is supportive during adolescence.

Imagine what would happen if either spouse were to die during a boy's early adolescent years. If the mother dies, the son's pattern of conflict might be truncated, and the son's development of independence might be delayed. If the father were to die, the son's development of his ability to resolve his conflict with the mother might be delayed, because of the absence of the father. For the girl, the mother's death may catapult her into conflict with her father without the moderating and supportive influence of the mother. The death of the father can retard the psychosexual development of the girl.

In any event, regardless of the stage of life when a death occurs, usual conflict-resolution patterns will be disrupted and the family will have to establish new patterns that help them survive the period of grief *and* cope with life in the later period when grief is less keen.

Commitment. The marriage covenant joins two people's flesh (Gen. 2:24). Death separates the flesh that has been joined. Sometimes, death of a spouse can make the surviving spouse wary of ever marrying again. After the death of a parent, the children may be drawn together into a more tightly knit family, or they may just as easily be torn apart, feeling the weakening of the fabric of commitment throughout the family.

Prior commitment within a marriage or family may create problems when that family must adjust to a remarriage, because part of the family's sense of commitment lay in the many shared experiences accumulated over the years. Those memories persist after remarriage. Talk around the dinner table may evolve into "remember our trip to Colorado?" or "remember when Daddy. . . ." The stepfather may feel excluded; nonetheless, the family *needs* to recall fond memories. However, one danger in such recall is that it is difficult not to compare a new marriage with a former marriage and conclude that because there are fewer memories in the new marriage, it must necessarily involve less commitment. Further, the new spouse is often keenly aware that there are few shared memories within the new relationship and can feel inadequate as a result.

Regardless of the form it takes, all family members experience disruptions in their commitment within the family and often in their commitment to God. They may also compare the commitment of new relationships to the memory of the commitment within former relationships. These bonds of commitment must be strengthened or others must be forged.

THE SOCIOLOGY OF DIVORCE

Family sociologists have speculated about social factors associated with divorce. One of the most complete theories relevant to predicting likelihood of divorce was proposed by Levinger[5] and modified and expanded by Lewis and Spanier.[6] Generally, the model assumes that marital stability is affected by three types of forces: attractions between partners, perceived barriers to divorce, and alternatives that draw the partners apart. I have represented this model pictorially in Figure 6–1.

Attractions for Remaining Married

Relationship quality. The quality of the relationship depends on the net rewards of the relationship weighed against the

**Sociological Factors Increasing
and Decreasing Marital Stability**

BARRIERS
- Religion
- Children
- Legal hassles and costs
- Loss of economic status
- Commitment to marital bond
- Community stigma
- Family-of-origin influences
- Fear of AIDS and STD

ATTRACTIONS
- Marital quality
- Companionship
- Sexual pleasure
- Income
- Home ownership
- Education
- Similarities (race, religion, education, age, interests)

ALTERNATIVES
- Employment of wife
- Single life
- Sources of affection

Sources: Levinger (1965); Lewis & Spanier (1979)

Figure 6-1

expected net rewards. When couples get more than they expect from their marriage, they report satisfaction with the marriage. High marital satisfaction is related to high marital stability, but the converse is not necessarily true.[7] People with low marital satisfaction may have extremely stable marriages because of the other attractions, barriers, and alternatives to divorce.

Companionship. One attraction between spouses is friendship. People who enjoy each other's company are likely to remain married.[8]

Sexual pleasure. While a good sexual life is not necessary for a good marriage, it sure helps. Most people with highly satisfying marriages also report a good sexual relationship, including more frequent orgasms for the wife relative to couples with less satisfying marriages. However, dissatisfaction with the sexual relationship in marriage is more predictive of husbands' dissatisfaction with the marriage than it is of wives' dissatisfaction.[9]

Income. Over the years, husbands' income has generally been associated positively with marital stability. As more wives have entered the work force at higher paying jobs, the effects of economics on marital stability have become more complicated.[10]

Home ownership. Couples who own their own home are less likely to divorce than are couples who rent or live in an apartment.[11] Home ownership can be an indication of commitment to the relationship and is thus listed under attractions as a force promoting marital stability. It can also be an economic barrier to divorce because the divorce would require property redistribution and other financial hassles.

Education. Generally, higher levels of education are related to marital stability.[12] Of course, many factors are confounded with the amount of education that the couple has obtained. For example, more highly educated couples have probably married later in life, bringing more maturity to their marriages. Further, they are probably more financially secure than the early married and thus experience fewer financial strains on their relationship.

Similarities. Similarity on a variety of issues generally is related to marriage longevity: race,[13] religion,[14] age,[15] socioeconomic status,[16] and education.[17]

Barriers Against Divorce

It is not just the mutual attraction of spouses that keep them together. External pressures usually force the couple together and keep them from leaving the marriage, even when troubles are encountered. But as divorce becomes more common within the United States and other western countries, the barriers to divorce are lowering, in part due to the sheer weight of numbers. If many people are divorcing, then others reason that it must be an acceptable thing to do.

Religion. Traditionally, religion has been a strong barrier to divorce. Roman Catholics have taken the strongest and most consistent position against it. Consequently, Roman Catholics report a lower divorce rate than do Protestants, though the rate of separation is roughly similar.[18] One might expect that theologically conservative Protestants have a low divorce rate given that there are often theological and social pressures brought to bear against the troubled couple wishing to divorce. At least in one study, though, fundamentalists and Baptists have been found to have higher divorce rates than have Roman Catholics.[19] Some social scientists have speculated that religious fundamentalism contributes to a rigid cognitive style and a focus on the afterlife rather than the present life, both of which make divorce more likely than one might expect by examining doctrinal positions of the various theologically conservative churches.[20] It has been my experience, though, that the religiously conservative person is no more cognitively rigid than is the religiously moderate or religiously liberal person—nor indeed than the non-religious person. Rather, the topics about which the rigidity is manifested are simply different. On the other hand, until recent years, religious conservatism has been associated with lower socioeconomic status, which in turn has been associated with less education, less income, less common property, and fewer social barriers against divorce. These factors might explain some of the research findings since most are associated with high rates of divorce.

Children. We rarely hear today that a couple is "staying together for the kids." Much research has demonstrated that, while divorce is difficult for children, it is not usually so traumatic that the child cannot bounce back after a time.[21] This finding and the recognition that spousal conflict, rather than divorce per se, is partially responsible for negative psychological effects on children have reduced the belief that remaining together in an openly conflicted marriage is better for the children than divorcing.

Recently, this finding has been questioned in an important longitudinal research study. Judith Wallerstein, researcher, and her coauthor, Sandra Blakeslee, have reported on a 15-year study of 60 divorced families involving 131 children.[22] The families were from Marin County, a financially well-to-do section of northern California in which education and psychological soundness were high. Families were interviewed at one, five, ten, and fifteen years into the study. At the beginning of the study, Wallerstein agreed with the common dogma that divorce was a stressful event from which both adults and children soon rebounded.

After fifteen years, however, she changed her mind. She now considers divorce to be an explosion that may send recurring shock waves through the lives of both the adults and children involved. At least one-fifth of the divorced adults still reported serious disturbance over their divorce after fifteen years. The children of divorce were often still upset by their parents' divorces, reporting anger, feelings of abandonment (especially directed at the father), and problems that exploded like land mines years after the divorce.

Despite some serious methodological problems in Wallerstein's research (notably the absence of a control group of comparable nondivorced families), her results must be taken seriously, because hers is one of the few studies to follow the same people for years after a divorce. Her findings may suggest that divorcing couples have sometimes underestimated the long-term trauma of divorce.

Postdivorce psychological adjustment of children depends on a variety of factors, including continued conflict between divorced spouses, psychological adjustment of the custodial parent, relationship with the non-custodial parent, childrearing practices, remarriage, relationship with step-parent if remarriage occurs, and type of physical custody (as opposed to type of legal custody).[23]

Despite the justification for remaining in an unsatisfying marriage "for the sake of the kids," the presence of children in a marriage still presents a significant barrier to divorce. This is often especially true for the wife, for she will generally be given major custody responsibilities and will often be earning less than her husband. Further, many husbands have defaulted on their court-mandated child-support payments, making the wife uneasy about her financial status and of her ability to support the children and herself financially should divorce occur. Many women may still contemplate ending a marriage only when the children are at an age at which the woman believes she can support them—e.g., after they enter school and she can work without full-time child-care expense.[24]

Legal hassles and costs. Getting a divorce is not inexpensive. Even an initial consultation with a lawyer might cost three hundred dollars or more, and if there is significant disagreement about property or child custody, then the only winners in a divorce case are the lawyers, who may collect thousands of dollars in fees. Other fees might be involved, too, for counseling (which could cost a thousand dollars for fifteen visits) or for divorce mediation (which is generally less expensive and less anger-producing than lawyers, but which requires that the couple compromise) or for accountants in making property settlements. To many couples, the economic burden of divorce is too high. Often one party will simply desert the spouse to avoid the financial costs and hassles.

Loss of economic status. Generally, two wage earners within the same household can live at a higher standard of living than they could if they were on their own. Divorce will almost always signal a loss of economic status for both parties.

Commitment to the marital bond. Individuals have differing commitments to marriage. The level of commitment can be affected by such things as (a) whether the couple cohabited prior to their marriage (cohabitors typically have a higher divorce rate than noncohabitors[25]), (b) whether either spouse has been divorced previously,[26] and (c) the number of years a person has invested in a particular marriage (people are more reluctant to end a long marriage than they are to end a short marriage).

Community stigma. When a marriage is known by many people, those people pressure the couple to continue in marriage. For example, in rural areas, divorce is less likely than in the more impersonal urban areas. In addition, Lewis and Spanier have shown that divorce is impeded when a couple participates in more volunteer organizations, is prominent in a community, and has more friends within the community. In some communities, such as close religious communities in which there is a community norm opposing it, divorce is rare unless the couple leaves the community. In lower socioeconomic status communities, the financial rewards of being single can outweigh the financial rewards of marriage, so the community not only accepts but may even support divorce.

Family-of-origin influences. Parents who do not divorce have children who are less likely to divorce than do parents who have been divorced. Parents rear their children in an environment in which norms may be taught explicitly but (probably more powerfully) may be learned implicitly.

Fear of AIDS and STD. Within the last five to ten years, the epidemics of sexually transmitted diseases (STDs) and AIDS have given rise to increased sexual monogamy. For some, the fear of contracting some sexual disease from a different sexual partner not only contributes to fidelity in marriage but also to a reluctance to ending the marriage and placing oneself in the position of finding a new sexual partner.

Alternatives to Marriage

Whereas attractions to marriage and barriers to divorce both act to prevent divorce, there are a substantial number of forces that might contribute toward increased likelihood of divorce.[27]

Employment of the wife. Generally, marital stability has been found to be related positively to the amount of family income—with one consistent exception. Women who have postcollege education and salaries that are high also have higher divorce rates than women whose education and salaries are lower.[28] There are a number of possible explanations for these findings. Women of higher education and salary may be more independent and autonomous in their personalities or they may simply have more power or resources to leave an unsatisfactory marriage. Alternatively, a woman in a high-paying, demanding job might devote more energy to her job and relatively less to her family, thus adding to the other dissatisfactions of her spouse and children. Still another alternative explanation would reverse the causality: A woman might first decide she wants a divorce and then she might obtain a job to provide for her anticipated independence.

Single life. For many people, the responsibilities of being a spouse and a parent interfere seriously with their desire for independence and freedom. They long for the foregone hobbies, pastimes, and activities associated with being single. They may believe that dating is exciting and relish the establishment of intimacy with many new people of the opposite sex. They may even be intensely career motivated and see marriage as an impediment to career advancement. In short, they may be motivated to be single as an escape from marriage or because of what they perceive as a pull toward the single life.

Other sources of affection. Most people are attracted to others at various times throughout their marriage. While marital infidelity is reported to occur in as much as 40 percent of all marriages, that statistic is somewhat misleading. Generally, among that 40 percent, the infidelity was an isolated incident occurring only once. Also, in many of those couples, the affair occurs after separation but before legal divorce, or during the last phase of a marriage that is already headed for divorce. In few cases do sexual infidelities actually occur when partners are satisfied.[29] Nonetheless, the attractions of an affectional relationship outside of marriage can be strong when the marriage is already under strain. Where their marriages involve dissatisfaction, spouses may begin to think about the suitability of other potential mates, whereas they rarely if ever evaluate their other-sex friends along those lines if the marriage is untroubled.

THE PSYCHOLOGY OF DIVORCE

Reasons Cited for Divorce

Although there are sociological factors that enable us to predict couples who are at risk for divorce within a large sample of

people, individuals do not explain their divorces by citing sociological factors. As we might expect, research has revealed that
the reasons cited for divorce during the 1980s were quite different from those cited in earlier decades. In a review of two major
inquiries into the reasons people cited for divorce, Price and
McKenry found that specific blameworthy behaviors such as
drinking, spouse abuse, desertion, gambling, infidelity, and lack
of interest in the home, were cited as primary causes for divorce
during decades past,[30] when legal divorce required a determination of cause. On the other hand, more recent studies, conducted
in the time of "no-fault" divorce, show the major reasons cited to
justify divorce to be lifestyle differences, financial difficulties,
sexual difficulties, personal incompatibility, communication
difficulties, value conflicts, boredom, the spouse's infidelity,
emotional and personality problems, drinking, violence, and im-
maturity, and (among women) the desire for more freedom.[31]
Price and McKenry suggest that marriage is increasingly seen as
a vehicle for personal gratification and that whenever spouses
perceive that their marital relationship is hampering their personal gratification, they are less willing to remain in the marriage than in times past.[32]

Stages of Divorce

People experience divorce differently. For some, divorce is a
mental-health-threatening trauma, while for others, it is a relief.
For most, divorce is an emotional roller coaster; but for a few, it
is an emotional flat land. Some experiences are common enough
to warrant describing them as "stages of divorce." A variety of
authors have described such stages.[33] I have drawn on some
of these theories and my own experience in marriage counseling
to suggest a typical sequence for divorce.

Closeness wanes. While many divorces occur after a protracted period of marital dissatisfaction, many also occur after
many years of satisfying marriage. In the latter case, often some
precipitating event changes the couple's experience within the
marriage. In both the protracted and the sudden (within about a
year) divorce, the initial closeness between spouses is eroded.
Perhaps intimacy declines after a normal life change—such as
birth of a child or retirement—which disrupts the couple's time

schedules and forces the spouses to rearrange their patterns of intimacy and distance. Or perhaps the change occurs because of some less frequent event—such as being laid off at work, death of a child, or onset of severe psychological or physical problems in one spouse. Or perhaps the behavior of one spouse changes in such a way that the other feels less intimacy. In one couple, the husband began to demand increasingly more un- usual sexual behaviors from his wife, until she felt alienated. In another couple, the wife had an affair with a co-worker. In a third couple, the husband's drinking increased until the wife felt "turned off" by his behavior.

During the time when intimacy is declining, the couple will often continue to maintain public behavior that suggests that they are a "perfect couple." Yet privately, they are becoming more disillusioned with each other. They begin to think about their spouses' faults and deficiencies. Intimacy generally has its ups and downs in any normal couple. However, its downs are now interpreted as evidence that the spouses' love for each other has drastically decreased or even died.

In many couples, the decline of intimacy signals a need to redouble their efforts to reestablish a close relationship. In those couples, the spouses often focus on how to love each other bet- ter. In contrast, other couples might dwell on the negative and focus on how to *get* love rather than how to *give* it. Overall, the attractions between the partners are loosening as closeness wanes and the relationship moves toward divorce.

Communication suffers. Jessie and Steven had experienced a decline in their feelings of closeness for each other over a period of about three years. Despite the warning signs, they continued to pursue their own interests and began to exclude each other from their lives. At first, they simply scheduled their lives so that they had less time for each other; but as time passed, the physical separateness was transformed into an emotional sepa- rateness. Steven described his feelings as if there were an "iron wall between them." Jessie described herself as "numb." At times, anger and hurt welled up in the relationship. For years, they had communicated well, but suddenly they found them- selves "sniping" at each other and having occasional "blowups." Jessie confessed to me that she felt that staying in the marriage was more costly than it was beneficial. As they discussed their marriage within my office, they continually interrupted each other with put-down humor. My impression was that they were "scoring points," trying to maintain at least an equality—or even an upper hand—in the relationship. They were clearly, to my eyes, in a power struggle.

Conflict management deteriorates. As normal communication falters, differences that were previously glossed over as unimportant begin to loom large and cry out for resolution. Conflict-management strategies that worked for years of happy marriage fail. For example, Scott and Joan blamed their difficulties on Scott's mother coming to live with them. At least that was when the difficulties began. Scott's mother was in poor health, smoked, and drank. Neither Scott nor Joan smoked or drank, so dealing with her had been a trial, especially to Joan, who performed most of the care. When Scott's mother moved to a nursing home, they expected their difficulties to cease, but the tensions remained. For years, most conflict had been resolved by Joan's expression of her feelings and Scott's willingness to accommodate. However, when Joan had expressed her feelings about Scott's mother, he had balked. The pattern that had worked for years no longer seemed fair to Scott, and Joan perceived his recent unyieldingness on many other issues to be unreasonable and selfish. The emotionality of their confrontations increased until there were few topics about which they could talk without an argument. Their conflict-management strategies were in complete disarray.

Commitment fails. After the decline of closeness, the degeneration of communication, and the bankruptcy of conflict-management strategies, commitment to the marriage has already suffered. The attractions of marriage have been decreased substantially. In the final phases of divorce, the alternatives to marriage are considered. Whereas spouses previously might have entertained occasional thoughts about what life would be like if they were single, in the final stage of divorce, those thoughts are at the forefront of the mind. They may seriously evaluate the benefits and costs of single life, even considering some of their single friends as potential mates. They may begin to flirt and to develop an intimate relationship with co-workers or friends. Emotionally, they may respond little to the spouse, no longer even feeling or expressing anger or hurt.

In other marriages, one spouse is the initiator of divorce and the other often continues to try to regain the lost relationship. But when one spouse has completely withdrawn from the relationship, it is often not possible to revive the marriage. My observation of the dynamics of many such couples' relationships has led me to believe that trying to restore the marriage is often simply a power strategy employed by the rejected spouse. The strategy is powerful in that it brings public opinion (especially within the church community) to bear on the other spouse. Further, because a "virtuous" stance is taken, the strategy protects the self-esteem of the rejected spouse, who can then righteously feel that he or she has been wronged and is not responsible for the marital dissolution. In some instances, I have seen such cases in which the rejecting spouse returns to the marriage. Often, this does not help the relationship, because the rejecting spouse may feel defeated and overpowered by the public and private pressure to which he or she has succumbed.

On the other hand, often one spouse sincerely wants to re-establish the relationship. In those cases, the rejected spouse may still cling to the hope of reconciliation throughout continual efforts by the rejecting spouse to end the marriage. The rejected spouse usually feels hurt more than angry in such relationships, though both emotions are common.

As commitment steadily declines, there comes a point at which the attractions of being married are nearly equal to the attractions of not being married. The spouse's thought life is characterized by ambivalence and uncertainty over what to do. Some people try to end the uncertainty quickly by initiating separation and by following the separation with divorce as soon as the laws of the state allow. People who rush their decisions to separate and divorce have been found not to adjust as well to the divorce as people who allow more time between ambivalence and separation and between separation and divorce.[34]

A giant step toward ending a marriage is taken when one or both spouses decide to separate. Separation usually signifies a public weakening of the barriers to divorce. It suggests to the couple that their commitment may not be permanent. Often the physical separation is accompanied by a legal declaration of the separation, and by telling friends and parents that they have separated. Generally, for the couple, the separation is the most stressful part of divorce; however, a few people report that their emotional state improves after separation.[35]

Some separations end in reconciliation. This means that the ambivalence generally does not abate simply because a decision is made to separate. The separation may intensify the feelings of attraction between the spouses by informing them about what they would miss by divorce. Or the separation may intensify the relief felt at the decrease of hostilities afforded by ceasing their daily contact.

Adjustment to Divorce

If the couple divorces, then each spouse must adjust to the divorce, which again may result in a rather predictable sequence of experiences. In about one-sixth of divorces, people describe their reactions as positive,[36] but in most cases, divorce is perceived as extremely stressful, almost as stressful as the death of a spouse. Disruptions can occur in the person's psychological, behavioral, and social functioning,[37] and for those who must continue to deal with a hostile ex-spouse over child support, visitation, or financial matters, the effects of divorce might be even more stressful than death of a spouse.

Psychologically, the person may experience depression, anger, a sense of failure, a sense of loss and mourning akin to loss of a spouse by death, loss of self-esteem, disruption of identity, feelings of unattractiveness, rejection, hopelessness, helplessness, and incompetence. Many of these psychological difficulties might lead to increased vulnerability to physical or mental health disorders.[38]

Behaviorally, the person may experience disruption in his or her home management routine, child-care and childrearing practices, work schedules, financial status, budget, health, and sex life. Old routines and behaviors are often inappropriate and new routines must be created and subjected to trials concerning their effectiveness.

Socially, the person may experience (a) disruptions in relationships with fellow church members, friends, family, and co-workers, (b) requirements to deal with the former spouse about property, child support, and parenting, (c) difficulty in dealing with a romantic partner of the former spouse, (d) difficulty establishing a satisfactory dating relationship or dealing with unwanted advances of potential dates, and (e) in general a lack of knowledge about how a divorced person should act (norms).

These adjustments vary with each individual. Price and McKenry reviewed a variety of studies and concluded that generally men experience more debilitation during the periods just subsequent to divorce but women may experience more long-term distress.[39]

Children and Divorce

Children can have a great impact on an individual's ability to adjust to divorce. An enormous amount of research has investigated the impact of divorce on children—so much that it cannot possibly be even summarized within this chapter.[40] Less research has documented the effects of children on the divorcing parents.[41]

In general, adjustment to divorce is more difficult under the following conditions: more rather than fewer children, male rather than female children, preschool rather than older children, and custody arrangements that are characterized by conflict (regardless of who has physical or legal custody). Like all of the generalizations in this chapter, not all families of children who fit these characteristics will have difficulty adjusting to divorce, but the risks of difficulties are higher in those cases.

COMPARISON OF WIDOWHOOD AND DIVORCE

Theoretical Similarities and Differences

Despite the similarities in losing a spouse by death or divorce, there are some major differences that will undoubtedly influence the person's subjective experience.[42] In both cases there is a sense of loss and a need to mourn the loss. Thus, in both widowhood and divorce, there is often a period of numbed shock followed by a period of search for meaning in the loss. During the search for meaning, the person may engage in obsessive cognitive and obsessive social review of the events surrounding the loss. Friends may tire of hearing the person recount the events and a strain on the social support system of the person may be felt. One obvious difference between widowhood and divorce is that in divorce, the spouse is still alive on earth, whereas in the death of a spouse, the spouse lingers in the memory as a "ghost" who is often idealized. Sometimes, the ghost of a departed spouse is more difficult to deal with than a living ex-spouse, because the idealization of the spouse can set rigid standards that are resistant to modification. Another difference is that the divorce may take longer and may involve more anger than the death of a spouse. Still another difference between divorce and widowhood is that people eventually *choose* to divorce.

Research on Similarities and Differences

A few differences and similarities have been established through empirical research on widowed and divorced spouses. Generally, divorced spouses have been found to have more serious consequences to their health than have widowed spouses.[43] On the other hand, widowed spouses have reported more distress after the spouse's death than have divorced spouses after separation or divorce.[44] This puzzling difference might have a lot to do with the people studied. In most studies of divorce, the divorcing people are relatively young compared with those studied in most research on death of a spouse. The younger couples may have fewer resources for coping with divorce over the long term. For example, they may have a less well-developed social support network and less financial security because of their youth.

Social class apparently affects the adjustment of couples to death and divorce. In lower socioeconomic classes, there is often not the stigma attached to divorce that is attached to divorce in middle and upper socioeconomic statuses (SES). A variety of studies have shown no differences across SES in adjustment to widowhood. It appears to be equally stressful at any economic level.

In both widowhood and divorce, there is usually a serious economic loss.[45] This is especially true for the wife. For example, Morgan found that 40 percent of widows and 26 percent of divorced women could be classed as falling below the poverty line at some time within five years of the loss of the spouse.[46]

Whereas divorce is perceived as stressful in about five-sixths of the cases, widowhood is almost universally perceived to be stressful. Generally, men have been found to be more psychologically reactive to widowhood than have women, but clearly both are affected.[47] Usually, in both divorce and widowhood, the manifestations of severe distress decrease substantially after four to six months from the loss.[48] However, individuals continue to be distressed for long periods after that. For example, when Parkes and Weiss followed up on widows four years after the death of their spouses, fully one-third of the widows were found to have poor or deteriorated psychological functioning.[49] Zisook and Shuchter also followed widows for four years and found 20 percent to be functioning poorly.[50] Wallerstein surveyed divorced people after ten years, finding one-fifth to still have poor functioning.[51] The effects of divorce and widowhood are psychologically costly for all involved. Most people recover within a year of the loss, but a substantial minority have long-term adjustment problems.

One hypothesis that has been consistently advanced to account for differences between those who adjust well and those who adjust poorly to stress is the size and quality of the person's social support network. Early research simply examined how many friends and relatives were available to help a person. Subsequent research has been more precise, examining the nature of the interactions between friends, family, and other supportive resources and the divorced or widowed person. In one study, Greene and Feld showed that recent widows with high support exhibited high distress levels, but long-term widows with high support exhibited less distress.[52] The authors speculated about instances in which high social support could increase distress.

SUMMARY

Relationships being torn apart, regardless of reason, create disruptions in closeness, communication, conflict management, and commitment. The divorced or widowed person often continues to be affected by the loss for long periods of time; the resulting needs can strain his or her existing relationships. The needs for succor can also impel the divorced or widowed person to seek a new mate. In fact, most divorced people remarry within three years. Especially likely to remarry quickly are adults under age forty and those with primary child-care responsibilities. Well over 80 percent may remarry within 5 years of the death or divorce. When remarriage occurs, many of the struggles dealt with before and after the death or divorce will be significant issues within the new marriage.

CHAPTER SEVEN

A THEOLOGY OF REMARRIAGE

COUNSELING PRIOR TO REMARRIAGE has seldom been addressed within either the psychological or Christian literature. Remarriage is a topic about which opinions are often strongly held and hotly defended, with many disagreeing about a proper theology of divorce and remarriage.

REMARRIAGE AFTER WIDOWHOOD

From the beginning, let me suggest that regardless of one's views about remarriage, we can all agree that in the event of the death of a spouse, the surviving partner is free to remarry (Rom. 7:2; 1 Cor. 7:39). In fact, Paul even encouraged remarriage when younger widows had children (1 Tim. 5:14).

Few would contest that a second or subsequent marriage requires different adjustments than does a first marriage. Usually, the widow or widower is older than the person entering a first marriage and may have an already established family. To treat the fifty-year-old widow or widower and prospective spouse similarly to two twenty-year-old virgins would insure that the premarital counseling in at least one of the two instances would not be well received.

Thus, regardless of whether you agree or disagree with my theological interpretation of the stickier problem of divorce and remarriage, there will be occasion to do premarital counseling with people who are remarrying. There is a need, therefore, to examine some of the special issues that beset such couples.

REMARRIAGE AFTER DIVORCE

Positions on remarriage have been broadly divergent. On the permissive end of the spectrum are those such as Small[1] and Plekker,[2] who suggest that remarriage is appropriate after divorce regardless of the reason for that divorce as long as the person who wishes to remarry is repentant. On the other end of the spectrum are those who are confrontive. They prescribe that the counselor declare that God's Word prohibits remarriage—if that is true in the instance under consideration—and remain unbending in reiterating the Word of God. A prominent advocate of the confrontive position is Adams.[3] A third position outlined by Virkler is based on the assumption that (a) God's principles are established with our best interests in mind, and (b) God will provide grace sufficient to carry out his principles if we are committed to him.[4]

The three positions differ in the balance they put on law versus grace. The permissive counselor allows grace to outweigh law in most cases of divorce, suggesting that remarriage, whenever the person is repentant, is thought to be allowable. On the other hand, Jesus admonishes us not to relax God's law nor to counsel others to do so. Thus, those on the confrontive end of the spectrum can also find Biblical justification for their position. A list of several biblical texts concerning remarriage is included in Table 7–1.

Scripture References Pertaining to Divorce and Remarriage

The Law	The Prophets
Genesis 2:18, 22-24	Ezra 10:3,11,19
Leviticus 18:6-18	Nehemiah 13:23-30
Leviticus 20:10,21	Hosea 2
Deuteronomy 24:1-4	Hosea 3:3
	Hosea 11:8
	Malachi 2:10-17
Jesus' Teachings	**Paul's Teachings**
Matthew 5:31-32	1 Corinthians 7:10-16
Matthew 19:3-12	Timothy 5:14
Mark 10:2-12	
Luke 16:18	

Table 7-1

Many conservative scholars believe that remarriage is permissible whenever divorce has been determined to be scripturally allowable. They often begin a defense of that position by citing Deuteronomy 24:1–4, in which Moses allows remarriage for the divorced person. Conservative scholars also cite Jesus' words in the exception clause of Matthew 5:32: "But I say to you that every one who divorces his wife, except on the ground of unchastity, makes her an adulteress. . . ." A similar construction is found in some authorities' versions of the text of Matthew 19:9. Ellisen[5] and others believe the sense of the passage implies Jesus' acceptance of remarriage if the grounds for divorce were legitimate because divorce without the assumption of remarriage would not make a woman an *"adulteress."*

Ellisen also addresses Paul's teaching in Romans 7:2 that a woman is bound to her husband while the husband is alive and commits adultery if she lives with another man while the husband is alive. He suggests that Paul was not giving instruction on marriage and remarriage, but was using marriage as an analogy to show that when we die to sin, we can take a new husband—Jesus.

Collins[6] summarizes a study of remarriage done by pastors of The Evangelical Free Church in 1980. They identify some positions in which remarriage is acceptable without relaxing the scriptural teaching. They suggest that, generally, Jews took remarriage for granted once divorce was final, though remarriage was always *allowed* rather than *commanded.* The pastors cite Deuteronomy 24:2 as giving the right to remarry once divorce is granted, Matthew 5:32 and Matthew 19:9 as showing that Jesus taught that habitual unrepentant adultery "dissolved the marriage covenant," and 1 Corinthians 7:15 as showing that Paul also took remarriage for granted in instances in which divorce was permitted.

Collins also points out that besides the exceptive clauses permitting divorce of believing Christians, the Bible does not deal with divorce among nonbelievers. Any divorce clearly saddens God because it separates the "one flesh" that the spouses have become through marriage. Nonetheless, if a non-Christian divorces, then later converts to Christianity, he or she is not prevented from remarrying a Christian.

Collins also stresses the fallen nature of humans and the divine forgiveness of God. Divorce and remarriage, when they are not biblically appropriate, are sins. But they are not unpardonable sins. When the person is repentant, God forgives and expects his followers to be similarly forgiving. Thus, *we sin* if (as Christians) we continue to treat repentant divorced and remarried Christians as second-class citizens, barring them from public services, communion, leadership positions, or full fellowship in the community of believers.

Many of these foregoing arguments will convince no one who is not already inclined to believe that remarriage under some exceptional circumstances is scripturally allowable. For our purposes in considering remarriage in this book, it is sufficient to agree merely that at least in the death of a spouse, remarriage is permissible. The following chapters can then be beneficial in examining many of the difficulties of helping prepare couples for remarriage. If the counselor believes that other instances of remarriage are also permissible, then the number of remarriages he or she may be involved in will be greater.

SAMPLE CASES

Sometimes the best way to understand the intricacies of theology is to consider individual cases that involve interpretation of Scripture. I have posed a number of situations below and offered some tentative ideas about an appropriate position for each.

Case 1: Remarrying the Same Spouse

"We are divorced," said Kathy and Jim, "but we would like to remarry each other." Kathy and Jim divorced because Jim had originally begun an affair with a co-worker on his engineering project. In anger, Kathy had retaliated with a number of short affairs of her own. Despite the pain of separation and later divorce and the involvement of family and church members on both sides of the divorce proceedings, Jim and Kathy had decided after almost two years of going their separate ways that they could not live without each other. They began to have sexual intercourse again and continued it. After the divorce, both had changed churches because of rejection by many in their former congregation. Recently, they began to attend a theologically conservative church together. The pastor suggested that they discontinue their sexual relationship, which they did. However, some members of the church suggested that it was improper and against Scripture to remarry the original spouse once divorce had occurred. How should Kathy and Jim be counseled?

Deuteronomy 24:1–4 forbids remarriage to the original partner if a divorced person has married a second spouse. God desires marriages to be reconciled, but when a divorce and remarriage are scripturally proper, then the new marriage is expected to be a permanent covenantal commitment. However, if neither spouse has remarried another, then a reconciliation with the original spouse is fully in line with God's purposes (1 Cor. 7:10–11). I would advise Kathy and Jim to remarry if they wish, but to reexamine their attitudes and nonmarital sexual behavior and to repent of their transgressions of God's law.

71

Case 2: Remarrying the Same Spouse Who Has Married Someone Else

Jon and Margo were married ten years before divorcing six years ago. They have two daughters in middle school. Jon now is married to Alissa, but his marriage to her has not gone well. In repeated contacts with Margo, Jon claims to have "fallen in love with her all over again." He wants to divorce Alissa and remarry Margo. What is your advice?

Deuteronomy 24:1–4 is explicit: A remarriage in this instance would be unscriptural. In fact, this passage states that even if the second spouse (Alissa) were to die, it would not be proper for Jon to remarry Margo.

Case 3: Remarriage of a New Christian

Robert and Courtney wish to marry. Courtney was divorced four years ago and has been a single mother since then. Robert has never been married. When Courtney was divorced, she was not a Christian, having only become a Christian two years ago. Because she divorced for what she now considers unscriptural reasons, she wonders whether it is ever possible for her to remarry.

Most conservative scholars argue that when the non-Christian accepts Jesus as Savior, he or she dies to the old sins in the pre-Christian life. The blood of Jesus has washed those sins clean. If Courtney confesses her divorce as sin, she is freed of its power over her and she is free to remarry a Christian man.

Case 4: Remarriage of Two Divorced Christians

Victor and Rhonda are both Christians, divorced, and anxious to marry each other. Victor divorced his previous wife because he said their marriage was bad. In fact he had had an affair that led to the end of his first marriage. Rhonda divorced her first husband after he had deserted her and moved in with another woman. Should Victor and Rhonda remarry?

This case presents extremely difficult issues for the Christian counselor or pastor to deal with. First, it appears that Victor's divorce was not scripturally permissible, so the pastor might have to decline in good conscience to marry Victor and Rhonda.

But what if Victor has truly repented of his affair and confesses that he believes himself to have sinned in seeking the divorce? Yet, by now, his first wife has remarried, so reconciliation with her is impossible. Should the pastor then refuse to marry Victor and Rhonda even though he is repentant of his previous sins? In my view, this question addresses the emphasis of the pastor on law versus grace. The pastor must wrestle with the issue before God. Is the remarriage a deliberate sin by Victor and Rhonda, or does the confession and repentance of the sinful divorce cancel any sin of remarrying by bringing it under the blood of Jesus? Even if Victor and Rhonda believe that the remarriage might be sinful, is it unforgivable? What would be the sin were they not to marry? As Paul says, would they "burn with passion" and be vulnerable to other sins?

I would treat the problem as one of discernment of Victor's and Rhonda's hearts and a matter of their self-examination before God. I would not encourage rushing into remarriage but would want Victor and Rhonda to spend considerable time examining themselves in light of Scripture and God's leading before making a final decision.

SUMMARY

I believe Scripture gives clear guidelines about remarriage in some instances, such as widowhood. And I believe the principle is also clear that if divorce is scripturally permissible, then the divorced person is free to remarry. In addition, several instances of scripturally permissible divorce are named specifically. However, Scripture was never intended as a comprehensive manual to cover all cases of violation of or exceptions to God's law. Because there is substantial lack of agreement, I prefer to take the position that on those points people must seek to (a) understand Scripture, its guidance, and its limitations, (b) remain humble about their inability to understand Scripture perfectly, (c) discern the will of God in specific situations through prayer, reasoning, and listening and looking for God's direction, and (d) act within their consciences while they respect others' differences. Above all, our theological position on the matter must be rooted in and guided by love, which may at times involve forgiveness and at other times involve speaking the truth in love.

CHAPTER EIGHT

THE DYNAMICS OF REMARRIAGE

CURRENTLY, OVER HALF OF ALL MARRIAGES IN A GIVEN YEAR are second or subsequent marriages.[1] The divorce rate among remarried couples is higher than among first-marriage couples.[2] Among the speculations about why divorce among remarrieds is so high is the belief that (a) remarried couples and families have more stress to deal with than first-married couples, but paradoxically (b) they prepare less for marriage (probably because they assume that their first marriage adequately prepares them for their second marriage). In this book, we want to understand the particular stresses of remarriage and how those differ from the stresses of the first marriage to help our clients and parishioners to cope better with stresses after remarriage than they would have if they had not sought our counsel.

In this chapter, we will examine some of the reasons for remarriage, the often unrealistic expectations about remarriage, and contrasts between first marriages and remarriages, along with tasks necessary in constituting a remarried family.

REASONS FOR REMARRIAGE

If you ask engaged people in the United States why they want to marry, they will almost always say, "because we are in love." By that they mean that they feel romantically attracted to each other. But the motives for marriage usually are much more complex that romantic attraction alone. People marry for a variety of reasons—many of which are unidentified and perhaps even unconscious.

In a workshop aimed at preparing some hundred couples for their first marriages, I asked each person to list reasons for marriage, other than their mutual romantic attraction. Their responses are listed in Table 8–1. Remarriage involves many of the same reasons, but additional motives also may play a part. For example, some people may simply find the single life intolerable. Many previously married people with children wish to remarry quickly because they are unable to handle or financially support the children by themselves.

Others have more psychological reasons for remarriage. Some people feel like failures after divorce; they want to undo the disastrous first marriage and "get it right this time." Others have suffered social censure from important people such as parents or church members, and want to remarry and regain the esteem of those people. Often divorced people will remarry, change churches, and keep their remarriage secret so that members of the new church will accept them. Others hope to reestablish the relative stability of married life that was disrupted by illness and death of the spouse.

I recall one couple who had been advised not to remarry because they appeared to be marrying for the "wrong" reasons. The pastor believed the woman wanted to marry because she saw the new mate as a financial rescuer for her and her three children. The man wanted to marry because he felt uncomfortable caring for his two young sons and he wanted the help of a mother. This was a mature couple, however, and they were not

Reasons for Marriage

- sexual attraction
- desire for approval
- security
- fear
- loneliness
- pressure from parents
- society expects marriage
- economic security
- it will help me be more responsible
- my spouse will take care of me
- I can lean on my spouse
- I can dominate my spouse
- together our strengths make us powerful
- we can have children
- my spouse is like one of my parents
- she is pregnant
- we have many common interests
- my partner loves me
- I love my partner
- my partner is my friend
- physical attraction
- my partner is my ideal of an other-sex person
- my partner cares about me
- we have similar values
- we talk about things that I have never previously discussed with another person
- we never argue
- I can get away from home
- my partner is good at love-making
- she had an abortion and I feel guilty
- we're living together and deep down I think that's wrong

Table 8-1

entering marriage lightly. The pastor's oversimplification of their motives hurt them and created ill feelings between them and the pastor, who viewed their insistence to go on with the marriage as a challenge to his pastoral authority.

COMMON MISCONCEPTIONS ABOUT REMARRIAGE

Visher and Visher[3] label commonly held misperceptions about remarriage "myths," and compare them to the "mirages of [first] marriage" proposed two decades earlier by Lederer and Jackson.[4] Some of these myths are described here.

Myth: Love and Caring Will Develop Instantaneously

Romance is often present at the beginning of the relationship, but love takes time to grow. Complicating the growth of love and caring is the presence of children. It is not reasonable to expect that one will love the children just because one loves the parent. For one thing, the children may not love the step-parent. Stepparents are often only tolerated (or worse, not even accepted) by the children, who might have issues of power and control with their biological parent, which they solve by with-holding love and affection from the new stepparent. Resent-ment may be felt if the stepparent does not guess what the child wants. One teen said, "My real mom always tucked me in and prayed with me. This one just tells me not to forget my prayers. I know I'm sixteen, but I loved those quiet times with Mom." The stepmother may be longing for quiet times with the teen but is hesitant to treat her as a young child.

Myth: Working Hard Prevents the Development of a "Wicked Stepmother"

Almost everyone in the United States is raised knowing the fairy tales of *Cinderella, Snow White,* and *Hansel and Gretel,* which have one thing in common—a wicked stepmother. One might wonder from reading children's literature whether there ever was a good stepmother. Stepmothers often try extremely hard to avoid being a wicked stepmother. "I'll make fresh cherry pie tonight and chocolate quiche tomorrow. Then I'll rearrange the toy room, paint the den, and. . . ." Often this causes rather than alleviates difficulties. The child thinks, "Why can't she relax?" The development of a stepmother-stepchild relationship is like the development of any other relationship. It is hard work, and it cannot be accomplished overnight. Sometimes what is needed is simply time and consistent love. Unfortunately, some step-relationships will never be harmonious.

Myth: Withdrawing a Child from a Biological Parent Enhances the Relationship with the Stepparent of the Same Sex

Combating this myth is research that has found that contact with the biological father tends to enhance the ability of the child to form a good relationship with the stepfather.[5] Step-mothers have a harder time than do stepfathers,[6] especially in developing a relationship with their stepdaughters.[7] Visher and Visher[8] cite clinical experience indicating when girl children are cut off from their biological mothers, they typically reject the stepmother.

Myth: Anything Negative That Happens Is a Result of Being in a Stepfamily

When Susan flunked out of college, she blamed her failure on being a product of a broken home. Her father had remarried when she was a junior in high school, and she had never liked her stepmother. When she left home to go to college, she believed her troubles would end. Susan believed her stepmother was responsible for her poor academic performance during two and one-half years of college. Her experience is not entirely uncommon. Children—and spouses—often blame their difficulties and troubles on their living situations. When the person uses his or her family background as an excuse to avoid taking positive action to make the situation better, this "myth" becomes a cause for concern. Well-functioning families usually have well-functioning children, whether there are two once-married parents, one single parent, or two remarried parents.[9] Further, if a marriage is in trouble, whether the marriage is a first marriage or a remarriage, the couple must usually work actively to resolve their differences if the marriage is to change. In either case, blaming one's family background will not help solve any problems faced by the children or parents.

Myth: Love Is Finite

Many people believe that the amount of love one can give is limited. It is as if we had a hundred love points. If we use up fifty on stepchildren, then there will only be fifty left for the biological children. Love is multiplicative, not additive: The more we love, the more we are able to love others.

Myth: Preparing Adequately Through Classes and Reading Will Prevent the Emergence of Jealousy, Anger, Rejection, and Guilt

Information about potential stressors is usually not enough to prevent experiencing hardships. (Otherwise, the well-informed psychologist would always be happy!) Information can help people manage stress by letting them know what to expect, by assuring them of what is "normal," and by providing information about resources they can use to cope with stress, but information alone will not prevent all problems. When people master information about remarriage and still experience problems, they sometimes attribute failure to themselves, which might lead them to suffer additional problems.

Myth: Forming a Stepfamily After Death Is Much Easier Than Forming a Stepfamily After a Divorce

Regardless of whether the remarriage involves widowhood or divorce, the adjustments will be taxing on all family members. Family members' expectations about what they are looking for in a family may fall into two categories: The divorced will seek a different family than before, while the widowed will often seek a similar family. This is especially true if the widowed spouse or children idealize the deceased adult.

Myth: Being a Part-Time Stepparent Is Easier Than Being a Full-Time Stepparent

In fact, it is usually more difficult to be a part-time stepparent than a full-time stepparent. True, the demands on one's time and the responsibilities are less, but in the part-time instance, the continuity of child rearing is disrupted and often the parent-child bonds are less strong.

TYPES OF REMARRIAGES

In first marriages, the partners may have a variety of backgrounds. They may have dated seriously, or they may have cohabited prior to marriage—or they may have been separated by great distances. They may differ in age, socioeconomic status, sexual experience, ethnicity, race, religion, or values. Adjustments to married life are great.

79

Every remarriage can have the same differences between partners as first marriages—and more, depending on: (a) the presence of children and (b) at least one previous marriage in the couple's history, which solidifies expectations.

Simple Remarriage

When a childless couple divorces or when one spouse from a childless couple dies, the remaining spouse might remarry another person who has not had children. In that instance, the couple must adjust to each other without having to deal with the instant family that occurs whenever children are involved. Obviously, that adjustment will usually be smoother than if the same couple had to adjust to each other while they also juggled the responsibilities of child care and discipline. Yet, the simple remarriage involves at least one marital history, possibly two, with powerful emotional experiences that people will try either to reproduce or avoid.

Remarriage with a Stepfather

When a divorced or widowed mother marries and the husband becomes a stepfather, the family will often have less trouble adjusting than in other remarriages that involve stepchildren. The boy children often respond favorably to having a stepfather, even if the boys still have substantial contact with their biological father. Generally, boys have lost substantial contact with the father (through divorce or death) and the presence of a new male figure in the family is readily accepted. Girl children usually identify most strongly with their mother, so that important relationship is intact in the stepfather family.

Remarriage with a Stepmother

Marriages in which the mother is the stepparent are usually significantly more stressful than are remarriages in which the father is the stepparent.[10] For girls, the loss of the biological mother may generate a feeling of competitiveness with the stepmother,[11] causing high levels of stress.[12] The problem is not usually as acute when the child is a boy, because his relationship with his father is likely to be more important than is his relationship with his mother.

Complex Stepfamilies

Complex stepfamilies are those in which there are children from both the father's and the mother's previous marriage. White and Booth found that complex stepfamilies are the most likely to end in divorce.[13] In many cases, the mother's children live with her while the father's children are noncustodial, frequently moving in and out of the complex family. The complex stepfamily often strains to cope with unstable time schedules, financial obligations, and possible life-cycle discrepancies. Further, there are two sets of family traditions and family expectations, which complicate the formation of a new family system. Ages of the children are likely to overlap, creating step-sibling rivalries and more strongly forged subgroup boundaries than in simple stepfamilies or those in which only one parent is a stepparent. Disciplining children can cause friction if the discipline practices are not uniform for children from different family backgrounds. For example, if Bill and Kate remarry and each has a ten-year-old boy, problems can arise if Bill spanks his son but Kate never spanks hers.

His, Hers, and Ours

Complex stepfamilies can also have children that come from the union of the remarried couple. Usually, these new children will relieve tension.[14] But that is not always the case.[15] Generally, when a remarried couple has a biological child from their union, the father's position in the family is strengthened.

Hobart identified five types of stepfamilies based on whether children were his living with the couple, his not living with the couple, hers living with the couple, hers not living with the couple, and theirs (assumed to be living with the couple).[16] He interviewed 232 families, including 94 remarried spouses and 138 first-married spouses (for comparison). Each spouse had up to 7 children in his or her care. Each family member also completed a questionnaire.

Five major hypotheses about parent-child relationships were tested. First, he found that both parents had better relationships with their shared children than with their nonshared children—whether step- or natural children. Second, he found that mothers had more positive relationships with their biological children than with their stepchildren. Fathers did not show the same pattern, presumably because the mother is usually the primary caregiver of the children. Third, mothers were found to have less positive relationships with their stepchildren than fathers had with their stepchildren. Fourth, stepparents had less positive relationships with older nonshared children than with younger nonshared (with another family) children. Further, that difference was wider than the similar difference found in first-married couples. Fifth, stepparents did not have less positive relationships with male than with female children, which was in contrast to previous research.[17]

Hobart also investigated the effects of his, hers, and their children on the spousal bond. He found that the most positive effect on the spousal relationship was associated with their children, followed in order by her children and his children. He concluded that shared children were usually a boon to the remarried family's relationships. However, the mother's children were more important to family relationships than were the father's children.

DIFFERENCES BETWEEN STEP- AND INITIAL FAMILIES

A lot of research has identified some important differences between remarriages and first marriages. Most of the differences seem to make it difficult for remarriage to succeed. Many of the trials of remarriage will have to be faced by the couple who are remarrying, and it is usually better to enter remarriage knowing what might lie ahead than to enter it thinking it will be all kisses and flowers.

Differences in Marital Satisfaction and Stability

At the outset, the couple should know that marital satisfaction in remarriage is likely to be (on the average) about the same as in first marriages.[18] However, remarriages are more likely to end in divorce—and in shorter periods of time—than are first marriages.[19]

Differences Due to the People Remarrying

Some differences between first and remarriages are simply due to the differences in people who are involved. For instance, remarried spouses are usually older than first-married spouses.[20] Further, remarriages generally have more age differential between spouses. For example, in remarriage, the thirty-five-year-old marries the thirty-year-old, whereas in typical first marriages, the twenty-seven-year-old marries the twenty-five-year-old. The education differential among remarried spouses is also usually found to be more dissimilar than between first married spouses.[21]

These differences are probably due to the restricted "field of eligibles" for remarriage relative to first marriages. In first marriages, potential spouses often share common environments, such as high school, college, or armed service. But for remarrieds, most of the acquaintances of the spouses are married couples, colleagues at work, or people within their church (who might not feel it is appropriate to date a divorced member of a couple who had attended the church together). At most work sites, the ages of the employees are more variable than at most colleges or high schools.

Differences Due to Children

Being older than first married couples, remarried couples face different tasks with which they have to cope. Usually, they are in different phases of the family life-cycle. They may be more financially established than first marrieds, but they usually will have some children from the previous marriage, which places more financial demands on their resources.

The presence of children in the remarriage is a major difference between most first marriages and most remarriages. Visher and Visher say that remarried couples always have a shortage of time, money, and bathrooms.[22] These are not trivial problems, especially the dearth of bathrooms. In complex stepfamilies, major wars have been fought over one child using all the hot water or spending too much time primping while others queued up outside the bathroom door.

The remarried couple with children must begin immediately to deal with child discipline—often using two different sets of criteria. Their time is more occupied with childrearing tasks, leaving less time for the couple to get to know each other. Children, especially older children in adolescence, often have similar sleeping and waking schedules to adults, leaving little time to converse privately as a couple. Even the honeymoon is complicated by the presence of children. Generally, the remarried couple has either no honeymoon or a shorter honeymoon than does the first-married couple.[23]

Differences in Expectations

The expectations for remarriage are less clearly defined than are the expectations for first marriages. Couples differ radically in their ideas of such things as what role the in-laws might play in childrearing, how much financial support is appropriate to provide a former spouse, what is the role of the stepfather or stepmother in rearing the children, and others.

Boundaries are blurred within the remarried family.[24] Divorce severs all sexual, and many financial, interactional, and time-sharing ties, but it does not disrupt parenting ties. Thus, usually, divorced spouses must continue to interact around parenting responsibilities. Death of a spouse severs parenting ties, but there may still be interaction with the deceased spouse's parents about the children.

Further, as Hobart repeatedly points out, there are his, her, and their children that may be in-living or out-living.[25] The shared physical custody arrangements needed to accommodate all sets of parents (and perhaps grandparents) keep the children moving continually in and out of each household, making the environment seem disordered at best and often chaotic. "It's like a bus depot," complains one mother in a story about complex stepfamilies. "We fed one boy off and on for three weeks and took him to Little League practice twice before realizing he lived down the street. It was the Little League that betrayed him. My husband knew we didn't have any children in Little League."

Differences in How Marriages and Remarriages Operate

Remarried and first-married couples have been found to operate differently. For example, remarried couples tend to adjust to each other sexually faster than do first-married couples[26] although within one year of the marriage, there is no difference in sexual adjustment.[27]

A variety of researchers have suggested that "ghosts" of the previous marriage—whether it ended by death or divorce—provide standards against which the remarriage is measured, whereas first marriages are measured against parental standards.[28]

Several researchers have found differences in how remarried and first-married couples resolve conflict. Cherlin has suggested that both spouses bring established patterns of conflict resolution and views about their effectiveness to the marriage.[29] Being prevented from having as much time to negotiate their differences as do first-married couples, the remarried couple tends to employ unproductive problem-solving methods, including some that might have been employed in earlier marriages during the time when the marriage was in substantial turmoil. For example, one spouse might use shouting or cursing while the other might reopen old wounds.[30]

Remarried partners might be reluctant to give their trust easily to a new spouse. For instance, remarried couples have been found to maintain separate bank books more frequently than do first-married couples.[31]

Less inclination to trust might hamper the growth of intimacy. Larson and Allgood investigated differences in intimacy between 33 first-married and 33 remarried couples after one and five years of marriage.[32] They found that first-married and remarried couples differed in conflict resolution but not in affection, identity, compatibility, autonomy, or expressiveness. On the other hand, in a larger study, Peek, Bell, Waldren, and Sorell investigated differences between 106 first-married and 108 remarried couples.[33] Their groups differed on 12 of 15 measures of different aspects of the family. In all cases, the remarried couples reported more disturbed functioning than did the first-married couples. Remarrieds reported less closeness, adaptability, expressiveness, problem-solving, communication, emotional responsiveness, emotional involvement, and positive feelings toward children. Remarrieds reported more conflict, control, and behavior control.

Other differences between remarried and first-married couples include, for remarrieds, lower self-esteem that often occurs after divorce, less likelihood of a religious wedding ceremony,[34] and a shorter courtship period relative to first-marrieds.[35]

Summary

When two people with relationship troubles attend marital counseling, they often believe that if they could simply end their painful marriage their troubles would end. They fantasize about reentering the dating world, with its excitements—even though its uncertainties might be scary. Usually, the troubled spouses imagine themselves remarried. Inevitably they picture remarriage as better than the first marriage.

As should be obvious from seeing the differences between first and remarriages, this is not usually the case. With divorce, the difficulties of the troubled first marriage are switched for different difficulties in adjusting to remarriage. The known attractions of the first marriage are switched for the potential attractions of a remarriage.

I usually counsel the couple to be wary of assuming that remarriage will be any better than the first marriage. I exhort them to adopt an open mind toward improving the marriage they have, despite the cost, because changing also involves many hidden costs. As long as they are married, I try to help them save the marriage.

Whenever death of a spouse or divorce occurs, though, and remarriage is appropriate and desired, I want to help the couple prepare for and adjust to remarriage as well as possible. I try to do this with compassion, forgiveness, and grace. This will entail not only making them aware of the differences between first marriage and remarriage but also apprising them of the trials expected as they adjust to remarriage.

ADJUSTING TO REMARRIAGE

Courtship Prior to Remarriage

Adjustment to remarriage begins during courtship, which is usually defined as the period of dating plus engagement. Only a few research investigations have examined the courtship of divorced and widowed people prior to remarriage. Hollingshead surveyed nine hundred people.[36] He found that dating and engagement durations were similar when a never-married woman married either a never-married man or a previously married man. However, if the woman had been previously married, the duration of courtship was less, regardless of whether the man had or had not been previously married. Several investigators found courtship of remarried couples to be shorter than that of first-married couples,[37] although not all investigators have found that to be true.[38]

There tend to be three phases of courtship prior to remarriage.[39] In the first stage after the death of a spouse, the surviving spouse often does not date. There is usually considered to be a time that the spouse "should" be in mourning for the departed spouse. Although there are no explicit norms for the length of time this involves, most widows or widowers do not resume dating for at least four to six months after the death.

In divorced couples, though, sometimes separated spouses begin "dating" even before the divorce is final. Often this is done more to reestablish one's autonomy or self-esteem than anything else. After the divorce, many people do not date for several months. Although the same norms do not prevail for separated spouses as are taken for granted following the death of a spouse—in fact, friends might encourage dating as a way to get over the divorce—the separated person may dislike the typical ways that eligible "dates" are to be found. Singles bars are not popular with most Christians and many do not feel a part of community meetings of singles. In addition, most singles are trying to reorganize their lives after divorce, especially women, who generally have physical custody of any children. Whereas the woman usually becomes a single mother after divorce, the man often generally is just single. His parenting duties are usually less than the mother's and he has more freedom to pursue dating relationships. This is reflected in the finding that men often remarry in less time than do women.[40]

In the second phase of courtship after death of a spouse or divorce, the person resumes dating. Men may feel uncomfortable reentering the dating field after being married for years, but since they usually initiate dates they can thus control their anxiety. On the other hand, shy men might delay dating longer than do shy women because they are reluctant to initiate dates.

Because the woman is usually the primary custodial parent, she faces a more difficult set of circumstances than her male counterpart. First, the man who wants to date a single mother soon realizes that a deepening relationship with her will likely involve increased interaction with her children. If the children do not respond positively to him, the man-woman relationship can be negatively affected. Second, remarrying men tend to marry women who are younger than they are, placing more people in competition for the hand of a remarrying man than for the hand of a remarrying woman, who generally remarries a man who is about her age or only slightly younger. Third, because the children are often present around the house, the children may interfere with the mother's dating relationship. The mother's dating indicates to the child that the father is no longer the mother's primary romantic attraction. This can be threatening to the child even if the divorce has been long finalized, because many children hold on to the fantasy that their parents will reunite even years after the divorce. If the child is threatened, he or she might try to destroy the relationship by pestering the adult couple, acting out, or behaving as chaperone.

In the third phase of postdivorce dating, the couple may become more serious about their relationship and possibly cohabit or become engaged. Isaacs and Leon followed up on eighty-seven single-mother families for five years.[41] At the time of divorce, women ranged from twenty to forty-seven years old and had one to three children. An initial interview occurred about one year after the divorce. In another interview five years after the divorce, the women were classified as either dating but not serious, dating seriously, cohabiting, or remarried. In the study, the researchers measured the mother's relationship with her romantic partner and also assessed the child whom the mother thought to be having the most difficulty adjusting to the divorce at the initial interview.

Of the 87 mothers, 20 percent were remarried after five years, 13 percent were cohabiting, 22 percent were seriously involved with a man, and 46 percent were not seriously involved. Generally, younger mothers, who incidentally had younger children, tended to be more likely to remarry than other groups. Older mothers tended to be more likely to cohabit. There was no difference across groups for religion, race, education, income, number of children, or acceptance of public financial assistance. Once the mothers' age was controlled, psychological adjustment was not related to their dating or marital status after five years. Children of mothers who were cohabiting had significantly higher behavioral problems and significantly lower social competence than children in all other groups. Moreover, these differences were found not to be due to any child problems prior to divorce.

O'Flaherty and Eels surveyed 248 primarily Roman Catholics who had been remarried. Participants were recommended by either Roman Catholic clergy or by a project to help widowed, separated, and divorced persons bring closure to their previous relationships.[42] About 70 percent of the respondents were women and about two-thirds resided in urban areas.

O'Flaherty and Eels found that the median number of months dated prior to first marriage was twelve, followed by five months of engagement. For second marriages, the median number of months dated was seven followed by only two months of engagement. Couples were then divided into two groups—those whose first marriages had a courtship shorter or longer than the median (seventeen months). O'Flaherty and Eels found that couples whose courtship was shorter than average before their first marriage also courted about the same time before their second marriage. Couples whose courtship was longer than average before their first marriage courted significantly less time before their second marriage.

Stages of Remarriage

Papernow has identified seven stages of remarriage and development of the blended family.[43] In stage 1, the adults usually expect (or at least hope for) rapid love and adjustment. The children, though, usually assume that if they ignore the stepparent, somehow he or she will go away and things can return to "normal" in their family with the biological parents reuniting. Both parents and children are thus living a fantasy.

In stage 2, the assimilation stage, the stepparent is assumed to be part of the family, but the children and parents often continue to hold onto and try to bring about their fantasies.

Because the fantasies are at cross purposes, there is a realization that things are not "right" and a frustration about the fantasies not being met.

In stage 3, the awareness stage, the fantasies are often acknowledged. Family members may discuss the problems with other friends, a pastor, or therapist. The family is often divided along biological lines and conflict becomes more overt than in previous stages.

In stages 4 and 5, mobilization and action, conflict is intense and emotional expression is at its height. A stepparent, especially a stepmother with no biological children, is often excluded from the children's interactions, causing hurt, frustration, anger, and often damage to the self-esteem of the stepmother and to the relationship between the stepmother and father (if she does not believe the father is being supportive enough). The biological father is often caught between wanting to support his children and his new wife. The intensification of conflict and overt signs of division, though, may be the stimulus that impels a couple to seek help, often through counseling or support groups. Their problem-solving resources are mobilized toward trying to deal with the problem.

In stages 6 and 7, the stages of contact and resolution, parents work together to solve the problem. Often the united front offered by the parents will help ease the resistance of the children. Conflict, if handled well within the family, can suggest some solutions and the family members may begin to bond together emotionally as roles are redefined and renegotiated.

While Papernow deals with stages of adjustment to divorce that occur within a year or two of the remarriage, Carter and McGoldrick (1989) and McGoldrick and Carter (1989) take a long-term view of adjustment to remarriage—one that extends through a longer portion of the family life-cycle.[44] Their main thesis is that people never wholly "adjust" to the great trauma of a divorce. The intense emotion unleashed by this event must be dealt with repeatedly, and failure to deal with it at emotional "peaks" can result in a disrupted remarried family. While the marriage bond is severed with the legal divorce, the bond between parents is not usually broken. Despite the separateness of two households, the ex-spouses must collaborate in parenting their child or children. Thus, any time ex-spouses have discussions about money or children, a peak of emotional tension can occur.

Remarriage of either spouse can revive many of the emotions and conflicts within each spouse. Often the remarriage of a spouse will provide a shift in the custody or visitation arrangements, which sometimes necessitates discussions (and often arguments) about money and custody. Similarly, whenever one of the spouses moves, there is usually a renegotiation about the custody arrangements, involving further conflict.

Illness of either ex-spouse can reactivate old emotions. This is often a cause for jealousy and sometimes a stimulus for controversy between remarried spouses concerning what the role of the formerly married one should be in any care extended to the ex-spouse.

Finally, life-cycle transitions of the children, such as graduations, marriages, divorces, childbirths, illnesses, and tragedies, often provide the occasion for the ex-spouses and their remarried spouses to interact (and possibly to compete for) the children's affections.

In first marriages, the first year of marriage is often a period of intense adjustment, conflict, disillusionment, and turmoil. In remarriages, though, several investigators have described a longer period as being necessary for minimal adjustment. Hetherington, Stanley-Hagan, and Anderson (1989), and McGoldrick and Carter (1989) observe that at least two years are needed for minimal adjustment.[45] Dahl, Cowgill, and Asmundsson suggest that three to five years are needed for development of a sense of belonging within a remarried family.[46] McGoldrick and Carter listed nine predictors of difficulty in adjusting to remarriage.[47]

1. A wide discrepancy between the life-cycles of the families.
2. Denial of prior loss and/or a short interval between marriages.
3. Failure to resolve intense relationship issues of the first family—for example, family members who still feel intense anger or bitterness about the divorce, or legal actions that are still pending.

4. Lack of awareness of the emotional difficulties of remarriage for children.
5. The inability to give up the ideal of the intact first family and move to a new conceptual model of the family.
6. Efforts to draw firm boundaries around the new household membership and push for primary loyalty and cohesiveness in the new family (thus excluding all other members of the family).
7. Exclusion of natural parents or grandparents, or combating their influence.
8. Denial of differences and difficulties and acting "as if" this is just an ordinary household.
9. Shift in custody of children near the time of remarriage.

SUMMARY

Remarriages are vastly different from first marriages. Generalization from knowledge of first marriages to knowledge of remarriages will be a source of serious difficulty and unhappiness, for the reality of the remarriage will never approximate its false picture built upon the experience of a first marriage. This is important for remarrying partners and their families to know. And it is vital for pastors and therapists who counsel people prior to remarriage to remember.

Remarriages have some differences that make them advantageous over first marriages, but most differences make them more difficult. As a consequence, remarriages more frequently end in divorce than do first marriages. Yet many remarriages thrive. In successful remarriages, the obstacles to family stability are seen as challenges to overcome. The family is able to lay aside the past and cope with an extremely challenging and new situation—one for which society's norms offer little guidance. The following chapter addresses some of the difficulties with which most remarrying families must cope.

CHAPTER NINE

DIFFICULTIES IN ADJUSTING
TO REMARRIAGE

PREDICTABLE ISSUES MUST BE DEALT WITH as a family adjusts
to remarriage. This chapter summarizes some of these issues and
difficulties, including closeness, communication, conflict, and
commitment. Many of these problems have been foreshadowed
in the previous chapter. The summary presented here is de-
signed to help develop programs that assist remarrying couples
with their adjustment.

CLOSENESS

Initial Emotional Separateness

Emotional differences within the family are usually at their
most extreme at the time of remarriage. The spouses-to-be have

established an emotional bond, rediscovered intimacy, and are usually in excellent spirits as they fantasize about how the new partner will meet many of their emotional needs.

For the children, though, the remarriage may spell the doom of their hope that their biological parents will come to their senses and reunite for the good of the family. Living primarily with one parent (or at least sharing their time between two households), the children have experienced the loss of one parent from their home through the divorce. They now fear that they will lose the affection of the other parent to the new marriage partner. Given usual courtship behavior, they have certainly been deprived of much of the remarrying parent's free time during dating and engagement, so their inferences certainly seem reasonable to them. Children thus perceive a vast gulf between their desired intimacy and their realized intimacy.

Boundary Problems

While children (especially boys) often develop good, psychologically beneficial relationships with their stepfathers,[1] this perceived gulf sometimes leads to boundary problems within the family. A boy's positive relationship with his stepfather often increases the boy's perceived intimacy. Girls often do not fare as well, sometimes developing hostile and competitive relationships with their stepmothers when the father marries.[2]

The entry of a stepparent into the family presents a practical problem to the family. What will the stepparent be called? If the parents hold a strong view of the nuclear family, they may insist that the children call the stepparent by a familial title such as "Dad" or "Father." This can create strong negative feelings in children, especially in those who are older, because they feel as if they are disloyal to their biological parent. On the other hand, if children call their stepparents by their first names, any authority of the stepparent can be eroded.

The place of the stepparent in the discipline of the children is one of the little defined areas of remarried families. Most therapists recommend that the biological parents do most of the disciplining of the children, even if the mother is the biological parent and the father is the stepparent. This is especially true when the child is in adolescence. The biological parents may still have conversations about the best ways to discipline the children and exclude the stepparents, even though stepparents must also live with the decisions. If the family progresses to the point where the stepparent adopts the children, then his or her role in discipline is usually increased.

There is a vast difference between the single-parent home and the remarried home. In the single-parent home, the children often take adult responsibilities in providing emotional support for the parent (usually the mother). In the remarried home, supportive children usually lose that position of preeminence when another supportive adult is available. The child thus loses a sense of intimacy and a sense that he or she is important to the parent.

When children are shared in two remarried homes, the family environment often feels perpetually chaotic as children continually move in and out of the homes. These agreements are often burdensome to the child, and parents may rebel against shared custody arrangements because of the resulting chaos. If a close, nuclear family is a goal of their remarriage, this expectation will contribute to increased misery over the ambiguity and disorder that results in actually sharing a child across two families. Further, there is often a sense of threat that the child will suddenly announce he or she likes the other parents better and wishes to live exclusively with them.

Other Close Relationships

Of course, intimacy needs are not totally met by family members, even if two families are involved. Children, especially as they get near or into adolescence, often prefer to live with the family that allows them the most contact with their peers. Many adolescents will actively lobby to stay at one family's house simply because their friends are nearer. This may be true even when the teenager is satisfied with the other family.

Other intimate needs might be met by stepgrandparents. On a practical level, families must decide what to call the stepgrandparents. Are they referred to as "Grandmother" and "Grandfather," or do the children find these names a betrayal of loyalty to their biological grandparents? The wise parent and stepparent will include the children in such decision-making.

Conflicts of Loyalty

Loyalty conflicts abound within the remarried family.[3] The remarried parent generally feels two primary loyalty conflicts: between the new spouse and the children and between the children and stepchildren.

The first conflict is largely due to the bond between the remarried partners, which formed after the bond between children was well established. This attraction to the spouse is often perceived as disloyalty to the children. Whenever the bond between partners is weakened, the family often divides along biological lines and is characterized by exclusion of nonbiological members and by open conflict.

The second conflict, between children and stepchildren, is usually the result of guilt over loving the biological children more than the stepchildren—or loving stepchildren equally, or even more. The parent (often the father) who is a residential stepparent and a nonresidential biological parent is in a particularly difficult situation, because he or she feels guilty over spending more time and emotional energy on the stepchildren than on his or her own children. This can be complicated if the parent then develops closer ties to the stepchildren as he or she notices the ties to the biological children visibly weakening.

Visher and Visher note that at least one of the parents in a remarried family has had an intimate relationship with a former spouse.[4] At times, the spouse and the new partner join together against the ex-spouse. While this can unite the remarriage, it might also dilute the intimacy of the new marriage by focusing attention on the third person rather than on the partnership.

Children experience their own loyalty conflicts within the remarried family. One obvious conflict concerns their feelings of intimacy with their biological parents. Parents, vying for the child's approval or affection, might relax standards for discipline; as a result, the child learns to play the parents against each other. At the same time, the child struggles emotionally to please both parents; ironically the child sometimes resolves this conflict by emotionally cutting off one parent. Usually, this is not in the best interests of the mental health of the child, because the child then will have difficulty adjusting to both the divorce and the remarriage of the custodial parent.

Another conflict experienced by children of remarriage is between the biological parent and the same-sex stepparent. Children often fear that they will like their stepmother more than their biological mother, which they perceive as a sign of disloyalty to their biological mother and to their family roots. Older siblings may reinforce this by reproaching a younger sibling when he or she expresses affection for the stepparent.

Emotional Distance

Usually, the emotional climate within the remarried family is less intense than it was in the biological family. This probably bothers parents more than it bothers the children,[5] because the parents often hold the unrealistic expectation that the stepfamily will be like a new nuclear family. The common mistake made by many newly remarried families is to try to force the emotional closeness by either commanding instant intimacy (as when the stepmother insists on being called "Mother") or trying too hard to win the affection of the children by providing lack of discipline (which wins only lack of respect), by giving the child whatever he or she wants (which gives the child power), or by letting the child always have his or her way (which gives the child license to tyrannize).

Sexual Closeness

Sexual issues arise naturally in remarried families, beginning during the spouses' courtship. Because the memory of the biological parents as a sexual couple is threatened, the children may try to interfere with the courtship. Among many divorced people, cohabitation is practiced—even though it may result in decreased marital stability, poor outcomes in terms of children's behavior, and a weakened spiritual life. When the divorced couple cohabits prior to marriage, the sexual mores of the couple are certainly scrutinized by the children, who are also likely to develop positive attitudes toward cohabitation and premarital sex.

Sexual issues can be especially prominent in remarriages that merge two sets of opposite-sex, adolescent children. Casual dress codes, and bathroom and bedroom doors that often are not shut can be a problem when these opposite-sex adolescents are sharing the same house. Another sexual issue in complex step-families involving adolescents is the sexual competition between mothers and daughters for the affections of the new husband or between fathers and sons for the affections of the new wife. The proximity of an adult and a sexually mature adolescent within the same house is enough to account for an increased rate of sexual molestation of girls under age fourteen years old by their stepfathers as compared with molestation of daughters by their biological fathers.[6] One coping mechanism for dealing with attraction among family members is increased conflict, which helps create safe distances. Unfortunately, the high price of this increased conflict is continually stirred-up emotions.

Generally, the sexual issues that arise in families are controllable if the parents set firm limits about proper dress and behavior within the family. The mistake occurs when adults assume the children will somehow be able to work out their own sense of norms about their behavior without the parents' interference.[7]

Summary

Generally, issues of closeness and distance are plentiful within the remarried family; but in time, the family members will generally grow closer. Parents must be firm in monitoring behavior within the family, but they must not try to force a feeling of intimacy appropriate for the nuclear family. The many differences between the nuclear and remarried family will frustrate such a dream from reaching its fruition.

COMMUNICATION

Spousal Communication

Sara and Ben remarried. They approached me for help in some of their adjustments to the remarriage, particularly in difficulties of familial communication.

Sara's first husband, Douglas, had died four years previously of melanoma at age thirty-five, leaving her to rear their two daughters, then aged seven and five. She already had a college degree in psychology but had not worked throughout their thirteen years of marriage. After Douglas's death, she took a job in personnel at a local large industry, and she gradually worked her way onto the corporate ladder.

Now, at thirty-nine, she had met Ben, thirty-five, who was recently divorced by a wife who abandoned him and their three children, ages thirteen, eleven, and four. Ben was a successful engineer, with a recent appointment as a midlevel manager. After a six-month romance, they had tied the knot.

During their courtship, they both marveled at how well they were able to communicate with each other. However, after marriage, much of their communication turned from the intimate sharing of values characteristic of courtship to the more mundane forging of a marriage and blending of two families.

They found that their relationships with their former spouses still exerted substancial influence over their communication with each other. For example, Sara said, "I just keep wanting to talk to Ben the same way that Douglas and I used to talk. We hardly ever disagreed and we were always so comfortable with each other. We never had to struggle to make conversation. Sometimes Ben and I have to try hard to find things to talk about. We don't share a lot in common."

At the same time, Ben said, "I keep trying to avoid all the problems I had with my ex-spouse, Dorothy. There were a lot of things we could never talk about, because she was very opinionated and whenever I shared my opinion, we always had a row. I soon learned that it was a lot easier if we just didn't talk. Now, it's hard to break those old habits. I know that Sara is a different person than Dorothy, and I know in my head that it's okay for me to share any opinion with her. All the same, I guess the habits are too strong to be broken instantly."

They complained that many of the similarities they had noticed during their courtship had disappeared because they were interested in such different things. For example, Ben was involved in his career, but he had achieved initial success that was currently wearing thin. He felt he was putting in time more than making a positive contribution to a career. On the other hand, Sara was deeply involved in establishing a career. She had had no desire to work after college and when she was forced to enter the work force after Douglas's death, she found that she liked the stimulation.

Sara had been the youngest of four children and her parents were aging, with her mother and father both in ill health. Ben, an only child, still had vigorous parents looking forward to retirement. In both instances, the spouses were facing different life-cycle events. Had the children been in different stages of life—for example if one set had left home and the other set had been in preadolescence—then the life-cycle differences would have been exaggerated.

They agreed on one thing. In both of their previous marriages, they had worked out ways of dealing with their children through discussions with their former spouses. Now, even that was impossible. Both sets of children seemed to respond well to discipline from their biological parents, but they did not appreciate any disciplinary attempts of the stepparent. In time, that had led to each parent disciplining his or her own children and not the other parent's children.

Parent-Child Communication

Sara's oldest daughter, Natalie, now eleven and a preadolescent, had become Sara's confidante after the divorce. Suddenly, with Sara and Ben's remarriage, Natalie was being treated less like an adult and more like a child—at the very time when she was developing autonomy as an emerging teen with a self-concept as a "young woman." The striking difference between her relationship with her mother before and after the remarriage provoked her to act out. She began to smoke and got in trouble at school for talking back to a teacher. Her behavior toward Ben was provocative and rebellious, and she cut off communication with her mother. Part of my role as counselor was to help the mother reestablish contact with her daughter.

Stepparent-Stepchild Communication

Ben was having a difficult time communicating with both his stepchildren. Natalie was openly resentful. Marcus, now nine, initially responded well to Ben, but in recent months had become more guarded. Generally, Ben saw himself as inadequate as a stepparent, though Sara complimented him on his performance and Marcus privately told me that "My stepdad isn't too bad, even though he certainly can't take the place of my real dad."

These situations are typical of many stepfather-stepchild relationships. Stepfathers usually evaluate themselves as doing worse as stepfathers than do their wives or stepchildren.[8] Generally, satisfaction with the role of stepfather is closely related to the amount and quality of communication between stepfather and stepchildren.[9] Stepfathers' relationships with their stepdaughters are generally worse than are their relationships with their stepsons.[10] Further, stepfathers who felt that they could discipline their stepchildren with the support of their wives generally were more positive about their roles as stepfathers than were stepfathers who did not feel that their wives supported child discipline attempts.[11]

Sara's relationships with her stepchildren were also not good. The oldest, Ian, thirteen, simply ignored her. Maureen, eleven, was openly rejecting. And Robby, four, was generally tolerant of her, but was not affectionate.

Again, Sara's experience is typical of stepmothers.[12] In a study that compared twenty-four biological mothers with twenty-four residential stepmothers and twenty-four nonresidential stepmothers, Nadler found that stepmothers of both types reported more interpersonal conflict and more depression and anger than did biological mothers.[13] Generally, worse outcomes were found for nonresidential stepmothers than for residential stepmothers. In remarried families with older children, most conflict took place between spouses; whereas, in families with younger children, more conflict took place between child and stepmother.

Child-Child Communication

Sara's children, Natalie and Marcus, also experienced a change in their communication as a result of the remarriage. As Natalie became more involved in acting out, she began to talk to Marcus about any signs of affection he showed toward Ben. Whereas their conversations had previously covered a wide range of topics, now the conversations generally centered on the inadequacies of the stepfather and the poor family situation.

In addition, both Natalie and Marcus had been displaced from their position in the family by the merging of the two families. Natalie had always been the big sister, but now she was Ian's little sister. To make matters even worse, Maureen, Ben's middle child, was also eleven, like Natalie, and—horror upon horrors—she had matured physically earlier than had Natalie. Marcus was similarly displaced. He had always been the baby of the family, but now four-year-old Robby was clearly the baby. All this affected the way they interacted.

Child-Friend Communication

When Ben and Sara married, they moved from Sara's small house in Richmond's West End to Ben's much larger house on the South Side. As in many cities, there is a world of difference between the two sides of town. Sara's children changed schools and were uprooted from their familiar haunts, friends, and pastimes. Despite Sara's promises that they would visit old friends often, the hectic schedules of one high schooler, two middle schoolers, one elementary schooler, and a preschooler effectively cut the children off from their former friends.

The family struggled with unhappiness for a while. The younger children seemed to adjust most quickly to their new home. The two middle schoolers clung to each other for support, and although they grew closer and more dependent on each other, they experienced more sense of loss of their stable friendships. The oldest daughter soon became involved in new high school activities after first complaining of being "forced" to attend a high school that was a rival of her former West End school. But new friends—all of whom had been uprooted from their middle schools to move on to high school—soon aided her adjustment. After about a year, the children had reestablished friendships and were no longer unhappy.

CONFLICT MANAGEMENT

Partners bring to the first union two sets of expectations derived primarily from their families of origin. The old saying often heard among marital therapists is that there are six people in the marriage bed (two partners and two sets of parents). With a remarriage, we have a metaphorical mob scene in the bedroom.

In a remarried family, conflict is more probable and will usually last longer than it does in first marriages because more people are usually involved and the people have a more firmly developed idea of what their new marriage should be or what it should not be than do most people who are marrying for the first time. Divorced spouses are often governed more by the "should nots" and widowed spouses are governed more by the "shoulds."

In research I completed several years ago, and in my own clinical experience, I have concluded that some conflict is not only inevitable during the formation of a new marriage, it is also desirable. The conflict allows the couple to work out the blended family's rules. The danger comes only when the couple gets locked into a power struggle in which winning becomes more important than resolving differences.

Conflict will occur predictably within several relationships. Below, I have summarized some of the most frequent conflictual issues.

Spouse-New Spouse Conflict

There are at least two sources of conflict between newly remarried spouses in addition to the sources of conflict that characterize any marriage. First, the differences between first marriages and remarriages create uncertainty between spouses and involved children, and the uncertainty leads to a need for the creation of many family rules. In fact, the number of rules governing the operation of the remarried family may become so great that all the rules cannot conceivably be obeyed and certainly cannot be enforced. This leads to frequent conflict when the rules are violated. Children may feel that parents are arbitrary because only certain rule violations may be punished.

The best solution to this difficulty is for the spouses to keep the rule structure in the family simple. Only the most important rules will be enforced, and they will be enforced consistently.

Second, children in the remarried family provide a source of conflict. Mary Sue had three school-aged children from her previous marriage when she was widowed. After working for four years, she remarried Randolph, a youth pastor at her church who had not been previously married. Randolph was three years younger than Mary Sue. Both Randolph and Mary Sue interpreted the Bible to say that the man was mandated to be the head of the house. Before marriage, they worked out a clear agreement about how Randolph would direct the household.

After marriage, they came to counseling because things were not working out as they had carefully planned. Both felt that they had failed in their biblical duty and both were in perpetual conflict with each other and with the children. Essentially, two things had made their adjustment difficult. Most importantly, even though Mary Sue and Randolph agreed that he was to act as a father to the children, including administering most of the discipline, the children did not accept Randolph's authority. At first they were openly rebellious, often challenging his authority directly, saying, "You're not my dad. You can't tell me what to do." Punishment usually followed such statements, but over time the punishment only seemed to make the children more resentful and rebellious. The children began to be more passive-aggressive in their disobedience. They did not openly disobey (which would usually result in punishment), but they simply made "honest mistakes" or they "forgot" or they obeyed the "letter of the law but not the spirit of the law." What was worse, the more Randolph tried to act as their father, the more they excluded him from their life. They almost never addressed a question or a statement to him. They answered questions in one-word responses. They ignored him.

To complicate matters, Mary Sue had worked as an executive secretary since the death of her husband and she was feeling a great increase in self-esteem and self-confidence. It was difficult for her to allow Randolph to be the head of the house. His youth and his lack of experience as a parent were always ready reasons for her to feel critical of his behavior. She rarely usurped his authority overtly, but she clearly had mixed feelings about his failure as a father.

Sensing lack of support from Mary Sue, Randolph had begun to argue with her, especially over child discipline. From there, the number of topics about which they disagreed was rapidly expanding.

The solution to Randolph's and Mary Sue's difficulties was not easy. It rested on changing their view of "headship." They too clearly saw that continuing to force Randolph's headship as a parent onto unwilling children was going to have disastrous consequences in terms of the children's psychological and even spiritual development. The children were already near to renouncing their parents' Christianity because it was so harsh and unloving.

Randolph and Mary Sue renegotiated their understanding of headship to involve Randolph's leadership in family matters excluding child discipline. Mary Sue was placed in charge of enforcing the family rules and Randolph was charged with supporting her and trying to build a positive personal relationship with the children. Randolph and Mary Sue came to define headship or servantship as being subordinate to love, for submission springs not from obedience so much as from love. We submit to God because he first loved us.

The children were told that Randolph loved them but that he knew he could never replace their father, and he would not want them to lose the special feelings that they held for their dad. He also explained that Mary Sue would discipline the children, but that Randolph would provide for them and be there to accept whatever they were willing to give. (This was, Randolph and Mary Sue agreed, a fair picture of God's love for us in caring for and providing for us even before we respond to him in love.) This understanding allowed Mary Sue to discipline the children effectively. Over a period of time, the children accepted Randolph, and he gradually assumed more childrearing responsibilities without resistance.

Spouse-Ex-Spouse Conflict

In divorce, the legal system is usually involved, and for the most part, that system is adversarial. Divorce-related disagreements often drain both spouses of time, energy, emotion, and money. Prolonged legal conflict feeds on itself. The more one puts into an issue, the harder it is for one to withdraw. Thus, former spouses may argue for years over property, child custody, visitation privileges, and alimony or child-support payments.

At the root of these conflicts is usually a power struggle, which is usually due to (a) disrespect for the ex-spouse's personality, (b) a history of hurt by both parties and a failure of both to forgive, (c) differences in moral beliefs and philosophy, and (d) differences in childrearing philosophy or practice.

In short, while not every divorced person has perpetual conflict with his or her ex-spouse, most have occasional differences that require resolution. Often this can place a strain on the relationship with a person's new spouse. For example, one custodial stepmother, Kathy, plaintively noted, "I'm with the kids all day almost every day, but John's ex doesn't want me involved in negotiations about their upbringing. John runs off and fights with her, coming back so mad he could bite nails. Often he has made arrangements that throw my entire week into an uproar, so we end up fighting. It's one big vicious circle."

Clearly, this remarried family is not conforming to the reality of the life in the present family. Because she is affected so much by any decisions that are made, Kathy needs to be included in the childrearing discussions between John and his ex-spouse.

In a different instance, Margaret and Evan, divorced three years, had basic values that were about as different as one could imagine. Margaret was a committed Christian and Evan was openly anti-Christian. Margaret forbade hard rock music; Evan played War and Roses videos for his own entertainment and encouraged the children to watch. Margaret attended church; Evan made fun it. Margaret criticized "pagans"; Evan criticized televangelists. Margaret had many rules about proper behavior; Evan had few. Each viewed the other as being a harmful influence on the children.

Margaret had gone to court, trying to exclude Evan from seeing the children, but the judge had not decided in her favor. Now, conflict occurred almost every time the parents had contact. For example, Evan would fail to pick the children up at the agreed upon time, so Margaret would take them with her to the store. She would return to find Evan fuming in the car outside her apartment. Then Evan would retaliate by not being available when Margaret came to pick up the children at the end of the weekend.

Their constant battles ended only when Margaret stopped trying to exert so much control over Evan's childrearing behavior at his home. She accepted as true that she could not totally control the children's upbringing and that all she could do was to present a good witness to the children and allow them to choose their lifestyle for themselves. While that insight did not end the hostilities, it lowered Margaret's internal struggles and sense of helplessness in dealing with Evan. After a while it also resulted in fewer overt attempts by Evan to dominate Margaret.

Spouse-Children Conflict

In remarried families children often have more power than they do in nuclear families because of the structure of the remarried family. In particular, when parents are separated, the child has an awesome power to hurt a parent by choosing to reject one parent in favor of the other. Even if the rejection is not blatant, the child soon learns how to play off one parent against the other in order to get privileges that ordinarily would not be forthcoming. "We don't have to go to bed at 7:30 at Daddy's house" or "Mama doesn't make us limit our phone calls to ten minutes" might not persuade the parent to change his or her policy concerning bed time or phone calls, but it creates a sense of guilt and insecurity that perhaps the parent is a little unreasonable and that the child might love the other parent more. This can often result in loosening other standards that are not challenged so directly by the children.

Other conflict involves enforcement of family rules. The keys to resolving this conflict are (a) to avoid insisting on the stepparent's authority early in the remarriage but rather to let the stepparent-child relationship and authority grow over time, (b) to have parent and stepparent meet with children and establish that the stepparent has parental authority whenever the biological parent is not present, and (c) to allow older children to participate in rule-making that affects them.

When Kirby and I go out, we always meet with the children in the presence of the babysitter and say, "While we are away, the babysitter is in charge. If you disobey her, it is the same as disobeying us and we will deal with that disobedience when we come home." Ironically, in some families the stepparent is so unempowered that he or she has less power than our babysitter. If the spouses agree on the limits of authority of the stepparent and if the authority is delegated in the presence of the children, then many difficulties can be avoided.

Child-Child Conflict

All families have at least occasional conflict among the children. In remarried families, however, additional sources of conflict occur because (a) the children are usually strangers who are forced to live together, (b) the blending of the ages results in a loss of definition about each child's role and position in the family, (c) the parents of each family undoubtedly had different standards for discipline and different rules for behavior, many of which require change when the remarried family is constituted, and (d) despite the ideal that all the children should be subject to the same rules, this is rarely possible in practice, which leads to resentment among the children.

During the first two or three years, when the remarried family is trying to forge its own operating rules, conflict over the perceived inequities are inevitable. The biggest danger is that the children will divide along biological lines and will exclude stepsiblings and stepparents.

Remarried parents should not expect complete harmony among the children. Rather, the parents should establish clear limits about how conflictual negotiations should and should not take place. For example, Janet and David called a family meeting of their four children after observing that there had been several disagreements among them. David began the meeting by saying, "Janet and I could not help but notice that a number of disagreements have occurred during the last two weeks. We understand there needs to be a chance for you to disagree, in the same way that the adults need to work out their differences, too. We don't want to step in and try to decide anything for you. In fact, we believe that you children are old enough to be able to work out your differences in a mature way."

Janet chimed in, "We thought it would be helpful, though, to try to talk about how you go about resolving those differences. We have some guidelines we're going to insist you use to work out your differences of opinion."

"First," said David, "no bloodshed. We've had a hard time keeping the carpet clean." After the laughter, he continued, "Also it would be good to have no name calling, no hitting, and no swearing."

Janet said, "Also, it's better to ask than to assume you know what your stepsibling thinks. Remember, we are going to be living together for a lot of years, and it will be more pleasant if we treat each other with basic respect than if you look at our life together as just one big war."

"That's pretty much the extent of our suggestions," said David. "Do any of you have any reactions to that? Do those rules seem reasonable to you? Do you have any rules that you would like to add—things that really bug you that you'd like others not to do?"

Family-Community Conflict

Remarriage, especially when divorce is involved, can divide Christian communities, especially when churches react to a member remarrying. Nor is the conflict limited to local churches. I have seen several friendly meetings of Christian believers turn into hurtful discussions over the issues of divorce and remarriage.

I do not advocate avoiding such discussions merely to avoid possible hurt feelings any more than I advocate going on a one-person crusade to win others to one's point of view. I view discussion among friends as being one way we come to understand our application of scriptural principles to real life situations. Yet, our discussions must be infused with love and sensitivity to people who have experienced painful failures and crushed dreams. We must truly guard our tongues in discussions about divorce, and keep a healthy humility about our doctrinal positions.

COMMITMENT

For the family in which at least one spouse has been divorced and remarried, the question of commitment looms like a specter in the background. Previously taken vows have been found to be nonbinding. Will it happen again?

The person whose spouse deserted her wonders whether another desertion is possible. The wife whose spouse was repeatedly unfaithful wonders if she did something to provoke the behavior and thus whether that pain will spring up again in the new marriage. People who remarry after a nasty and painfully protracted divorce wonder whether the current marriage could ever become so destructive that they might similarly wish to end it.

According to Rusbult's investment model, commitment depends on marital satisfaction, alternatives, and investments in the relationship.[14] Building commitment to a remarriage involves all three elements of commitment.

Marriage Satisfaction

As we see, the demands of remarriage are generally greater than are the demands of first marriages (though demands of first marriages can be enormous). Most people who remarry think the benefits of remarriage outweigh the costs—at least at first. But the margin for error is less with the remarriage than in the first marriage.

One factor that may work in favor of stability in remarriages is that people who have been through a divorce generally do not hold as lofty expectations for remarriage as do most first-time spouses. On the other hand, widows or widowers may idealize the first marriage and thus make remarriage even more difficult.

Alternatives

The alternatives to remarriage may differ from the alternatives to first marriages. For most people, the first marriage occurs in their twenties, when they are active and involved with active friends. The circle of unmarried friends may be greater for people beginning first marriages than for people who are beginning their remarriage seven to fifteen years later.

One alternative to marriage is the single life. People beginning a first marriage may be lonely and ready to settle down. People who have been widowed or divorced, however, may have been living independently since the first marriage ended. They may have demonstrated to themselves that they could survive alone, making the alternative of the single life less odious than it might be to the single person. Probably more likely, though, is that the single adult, especially if the adult has parental responsibility, will find the life of the single parent stressful and will look forward to again sharing parental and home responsibilities and to a more lucrative financial situation that usually comes with marriage.

Investments

Investments are resources that tie the couple together. With the remarrying couple, a host of investments come prepackaged as homes, home furnishings, car, and other assets. Another major investment in a remarriage is the presence of children. When the remarrying spouses have their own children, the marriage is generally strengthened.[15]

Forging a new commitment is not something that happens with the taking of the marriage vows. In practice, commitment is forged over time through spouses finding each other trustworthy as they deal with the adjustments of remarriage.

SUMMARY

The remarrying couple is in for challenges, surprises, and joys of adjusting to their lives together and to blending their families into a new entity. This chapter has focused on the potential problems that might occur. In every case, we find that the newly remarried couple must work to build closeness, to establish good communication, to mold conflict-management strategies, and to forge a new commitment. The obstacles against successful remarriage are daunting. It is through God's grace and by early planning and intentional effort that it can most successfully be accomplished.

CHAPTER TEN

PROGRAMS TO PREPARE COUPLES FOR MARRIAGE

MOST FORMAL PREPARATION FOR MARRIAGE AND REMARRIAGE is conducted in the school systems as a course in family life education or—more immediate to marriage—by pastors for their congregants. In this chapter, I suggest a comprehensive program for preparation for marriage that is aimed at pastors and counselors who operate primarily within a church. My thesis is this: If preparation for marriage is left until the last several weeks before the marriage, it is likely to be ineffective;[1] therefore, effective preparation for marriage should occur in a variety of ways within congregational life.

The pastor or counselor is urged to draw from this chapter only the suggestions that fit his or her special circumstances. In general, I will outline a program that encompasses education, premarriage counseling, post-marriage counseling, and involvement of others within the congregation as social supports for the marrying couple.

EDUCATIONAL METHODS

Church Climate

Preparation for marriage and for remarriage begins with the climate of a congregation. Generally, a congregation that values love, communication, and commitment will reflect those values in its care for the married couples and their children. The congregation will have a variety of family-oriented activities, couples groups, family enrichment weekends, or family camping trips. Relationships will be valued and there will be an openness to resolving conflict wherever it occurs within the church. If churches want to help troubled marriages, the pastor and others must make it acceptable to reveal needs and weaknesses. This can be done by open confession, offers to pray for and with people after the service, and availability of counseling. A church that conveys a message that Christians are always happy and trouble-free will have little success in helping people deal with problems that inevitably arise during marriage.

The pastor generally spearheads this accepting, committed climate by modeling open commitment and caring in his or her own life and through publicly (and privately) pointing out ways that people within the congregation are helping each other. The pastor treats the congregation as an extended family, which it is since all Christians are adopted children of God.

Although the pastor initiates an environment that values marriage and the family, he or she is not wholly responsible for that environment. Members must follow the pastor's lead, valuing commitment, love, and care for each other, and rejoicing at being part of a living, functioning family of God.

Sermons

While not everyone who reads this book will be a pastor, many will be. One of the best ways to establish a positive value on marriage is to preach about it. Of course, one cannot and should not attempt a message about marriage every week. Nonetheless, the pastor should frequently remind the congregation that the church is the bride of Christ; the marriage metaphor is used throughout Scripture to convey our need for fidelity to God.

The symbiosis between spiritual and physical marriage can provide the wealth for many sermons, as pastors describe how God established marriage as an earthly mirror to a spiritual relationship. We use our experience of marriage to understand our experience of Christ. In a similar mysterious way, we use our spiritual experience to understand our relationship with a spouse to whom we have pledged lifelong fidelity.

One of the many excellent sermons preached by my pastor, Doug McMurry, concerned biblical principles for mate selection.[2] Doug took Genesis 24 as his text. In that passage, Abraham sent his servant back to his former land, Nahor, to find God's selection of Rebekah as a mate for Isaac. Throughout that passage, many biblical principles for mate selection could be adduced. One of those interpretations is that God will reveal to each person his or her mate as a direct and miraculous answer to prayer, as he did with Abraham's servant. Or we might interpret the text as saying the biblical way to mate selection is simply to desire to please God and to be willing to obey his leading.

Doug used the passage to demonstrate that Scripture could be approached from many standpoints, all of which we might decide is God's message to us. Regardless of the way we interpret it, though, Doug pointed out that we should seek God's message in light of the historical context of the Scripture, our contemporary cultural context, and the direct and indirect leading of the Holy Spirit. God has a plan for us and wants us to seek him so he can in love reveal his way.

This sermon educated congregants, including school-aged children and teens, about the value of marriage and the ways people can make a successful adjustment to it. Many parallels also can be drawn between marriage and spiritual development. I have summarized some of those parallels in Table 10–1.

Sunday School or Church School

Another method for teaching a positive value of marriage, while also educating congregants about some of the difficulties

Sermon Topics In Which Parallels May Be Drawn Between Marriage and the Christian's Union with Jesus

Topic as Related to Marriage	Topic as Related to Spiritual Life
The marriage covenant; the nature of a covenant; leaving the old life and cleaving to the new	The covenant God made with Abraham and its fulfilment in the new convenant; conversion
Closeness between spouses may vary over time	Intimacy between a person and the Lord may ebb and flow over time
Communication between spouses	Communication with God (prayer and reading God's Word)
Conflict management between spouses	Conflict within ourselves over doctrines (such as free will versus God's sovereignty); Conflict between us and God when we do not understand his purposes
Commitment to the spouse	Fidelity to God and the fidelity of God
Producing children within the marriage	Evangelism (producing "spiritual children")
Rearing children and helping them grow	Discipleship: nurturing "young" Christians
Divorce: Why God hates divorce (but may permit it under some circumstances)	Apostasy: the divorce God hates most of all
Growing old together	Growing old with God; contemplation about the meaning of our lifelong relationship with him

Table 10-1

of adjusting to it, is the Sunday school or church school program. Pastors, elders, or other Christian educators might offer special classes covering a variety of marriage-related topics. For example, a class in dating, relationship development, loneliness, or breaking up might be offered to the young single adults. Over the past several years at our church, our pastor and I have offered separate courses in marriage enrichment. Both times, the couples who have been attracted to the courses have been the couples who have been married within the last two years, so the course could be aimed at helping them deal with some of the adjustment difficulties of marriage. The group format allows lecture or discussion by an authority on marriage and it permits a forum for couples to share their own struggles and to suggest ways that they have coped with common difficulties in marriage.

Midweek Groups

One format for helping people cope with the adjustment to marriage or to an impending marriage (if there are enough couples) is to constitute a group of people who meet weekly to discuss common concerns about their future or present marriage.

Workshops

People often are not willing to commit to meeting regularly to discuss their marriage. Within the church (and indeed within our entire culture) we often have the idea that only people in desperate need of help seek such information and counseling. However, many people find it less odious to attend something called a "workshop" on marriage enrichment. The format of a workshop is generally more oriented to information-giving than it is to revealing secrets or sharing emotions, which often makes it more likely that men attend than if the format appears to threaten self-disclosure, revelation of intimate feelings, and occasional admissions of a less-than-perfect marriage.

Efforts should be made to expose the workshop couples to information about which they know little. Having a workshop that covers material that is easily available and already known will provide reluctant spouses justification for not attending future programs on marital adjustment.

Educating About Preparation for Remarriage

The church has a dilemma concerning education about divorce and remarriage. On the one hand, because God values fidelity and commitment, the church also values fidelity and commitment. Because God hates divorce, the church also hates divorce, and never wants to recommend and promote divorce or remarriage after divorce.

On the other hand, there are legitimate reasons for divorce according to Scripture; and Jesus and Paul (as well as Old Testament writers) taught about divorce. Similarly there are times when remarriage is appropriate, such as after death of a spouse. The pastor must strike a balance between educating a congregation about divorce and remarriage, teaching love, acceptance and forgiveness, and not encouraging divorce and remarriage under circumstances that are not scriptural.

Often the way out of the dilemma can be simply to educate the congregation through sermons, Sunday school classes, and workshops about the scriptural grounds for divorce and remarriage, and about the psychological adjustments necessary if people are faced with those life events. Sometimes, though, members of the congregation have such strongly held and emotional positions about divorce and remarriage that a straightforward discussion of the issues can be divisive. In those cases, the pastor or elders might want to invite a special speaker from outside to lead a discussion or present a workshop about divorce and remarriage. That keeps the pastor from having to make public statements about the issue that might damage his or her relationship with the congregation.

CONGREGATIONAL RESOURCES

Another way out of the dilemma of needing to educate Christians about divorce and remarriage without condoning it (when scripturally sound reasons are not present) is to use a lay counseling program within the church to educate people about helping others—relatives, friends, co-workers—deal with these issues.

Incidentally, the use of lay counselors also helps the church provide premarital and post-marital counseling within the congregation when the pastor does not have enough time to provide the counseling himself or herself.[3] This stretches the resources of the church and allows us to be a priesthood of believers who mutually minister to one another in need.[4]

Besides helping minister to those in need within a congregation, lay counselors also can be trained to help respond nonjudgmentally to people who are considering divorce or remarriage and can facilitate practical decision-making in light of Scripture. Lay counselors are often leaders within the congregation, so efforts of the pastor or counselor at educating lay counselors will usually repay dividends as the lay counselors share their ideas with friends and family members.

117

SELF-HELP RESOURCES

How People Prepare for Marriage

As many as one-fourth to one-half of first-marrying couples attend some form of premarital counseling.[5] If the younger generation of high school students who are attending family life education courses in high school and college are included, the estimates will increase dramatically in the future.

The numbers are not so positive for remarriage. Ganong and Coleman surveyed people from Missouri selected randomly from marriage records about how they prepared for remarriage.[6] Most (59 percent) prepared for marriage by living together. Only about one-quarter of the men and 38 percent of the women had some sort of formal preparation for marriage. Remarrying partners often do not attend preparation for marriage counseling because they assume they know all about marriage based on their first marriage. Others had bad experiences with counseling as their first marriages failed. Many Christians do not attend such counseling because they worry—rightly or wrongly—that the counselor or pastor will condemn their particular intentions to remarry.

Ganong and Coleman[7] found that most remarrying people got most of their information about remarriage from two sources: friends and reading material. Women were more likely than men to seek help and to rate advice from both friends and books as helpful, but the difference between men and women was less for reading material than for friends. Only about half of the people who attended premarital counseling found it helpful, although Ganong and Coleman suggest that this might have been because the more troubled couples were the ones who sought premarital counseling. It might also be because the counseling did not deal with the problems specific to remarriage.

One important way to prepare for marriage is to discuss potential difficulties in adjusting to remarriage with one's spouse-to-be, but couples reported doing this surprisingly little. When they did discuss potential problems with remarriage, they usually did not discuss the topics that experts usually think are important in making a successful transition to remarriage. A study comparing potential and actual problems rated by first-marriage and remarriage couples just prior to marriage and again four years[8] is summarized in Table 10–2.

As the table shows, first-marrying couples primarily are concerned with threats to their own relationship, while remarrying couples are primarily concerned with complications that result from their children and coordination of a multitude of schedules.

Marrying couples, whether first-marrying or remarrying, optimistically avoid the consideration of problems more than most objective observers might say they should. As Ganong and Coleman found, however, when they do consider potential problems, they are often helped as much or more by self-help resources as by pastors or counselors.[9] This should suggest that a comprehensive program of preparation for marriage and remarriage should provide access to a variety of self-help resources.

Books

It is usually helpful for the pastor or counselor to have several copies of books that clients or parishioners can borrow. There are many fine books on marriage, so I will not list them. I have included another list, for divorce and remarriage, in Table 10–3.

Workbooks

Counselors also might recommend workbooks that guide couples in their discussions about remarriages. Norm Wright has

Problems Rated By First-Marrying and Remarrying Couples Just Prior to Marriage and Four Years Later

	Prior to Marriage	4 Years Later
First-Marrying Couples	1. Money 2. Relatives (in-laws) 3. Jealousy 4. Communication	1. Money 2. Communication 3. Sex 4. Relatives (in-laws)
Remarrying Couples	1. Money 2. Recreation (job, child care, visitation) 3. Relatives (children and ex-spouses) 4. Communication	1. Communication 2. Sex 3. Recreation 4. Money

Table 10-2

Recommended Books About Divorce and Remarriage

Bustanoby, A. (1978). *But I Didn't Want a Divorce.* Grand Rapids, Mich.: Zondervan.

Cerling, C. (1988). *Remarriage: Opportunity to Grow.* Old Tappan, N.J.: Fleming H. Revell.

Einstein, E. (1982). *The Stepfamily: Living, Loving and Learning.* New York: Macmillan.

Ellisen, S. A. (1977). *Divorce and Remarriage in the Church.* Grand Rapids, Mich.: Zondervan.

Frydenger, T., and **Frydenger, A.** (1986). *The Blended Family.* Grand Rapids, Mich.: Zondervan.

Hocking, D. (1983). *Marrying Again.* Old Tappan, N.J.: Fleming H. Revell.

Johnson, C. (1989). *How to Blend a Family.* Grand Rapids, Mich.: Zondervan.

Kysar, R., and **Kysar, M.** (1978). *The Asundered: Biblical Teachings on Marriage, Divorce and Remarriage.* Atlanta: John Knox Publishing.

Mumford, A. R. (1976). *By Death or Divorce, It Hurts to Lose.* Denver: Accent Publications.

O'Donovan, O. (1978). *Marriage and Permanence.* Brancote, England: Grove Books.

Smalley, G. (1984). *The Job of Committed Love.* Grand Rapids, Mich.: Zondervan.

Stott, J. (1984). *Marriage and Divorce.* Downers Grove, Ill.: InterVarsity Press.

Streeter, C. (1986). *Finding Your Place After Divorce: How Women Can Find Healing.* Grand Rapids, Mich.: Zondervan.

Thompson, D. (1989). *Counseling and Divorce,* Vol. 18, Resources for Christian Counseling. Dallas: Word.

Thompson, M. E. (1985). *Starting Over Single.* Burnsville, Minn.: Prince of Peace Publishing.

Wheat, E., and **Perkins, G. O.** (1988). *The First Years of Forever.* Grand Rapids, Mich.: Zondervan. (also in audiotape)

Table 10-3

compiled such a workbook aimed at couples who intend to re-marry.[10] It gives a minimum of information but provides questions that couples can answer separately and then discuss. The questions address some of the major adjustments of remarriage, such as expectations of the partner and of the couple, goals, roles, and responsibilities, decision-making, in-law relationships, communication, conflict resolution, finances, and sex. Wright provides a number of scriptural references to guide a couple's exploration of these issues, and he makes suggestions for other related reading.

Other Resources

Unfortunately, not everyone likes to read—a source of great consternation to those of us who like to write. At the present, though, most self-help material for preparing for marriage, and especially for preparing specifically for remarriage, is in print.

One of the inventions that will have a great impact on future generations of Americans is the videotape player. Most middle- and upper-socioeconomic class families have VCRs now and more get them each year. As a result, the general public is moving toward educational videotapes as a source of information. It seems only reasonable to expect, then, that high-quality videotapes about preparation for marriage and remarriage are needed to educate Christian couples about the adjustments they are undertaking with marriage or remarriage.

Such videotapes will likely be needed for family life education curricula in schools throughout the United States in future years. Churches should also own several copies of such videotapes for use in educational programs and for lending to couples. This would allow couples to view and discuss privately topics that may be difficult to talk about in a group.

So, here is my fantasy: A series of such high-quality tapes might be created, integrating current psychological knowledge and sound morals derived from scriptural principles. The series might show individuals, couples, and families how to negotiate many common transitions of life: to young adulthood, through courtship, to marriage, and to parenthood. Other transitions could be explored, such as the transition to parenting school-aged children and adolescents. Companion tapes could describe the transition to the empty nest, negotiating the mid-life crisis, career changes, divorce, the transition to remarriage, retirement, managing after the death of a loved one, and dealing with one's own approaching death.

Audiotapes

A series of audiotapes similar to the videotapes described above might be created which prepare people for life transitions, in the present case preparation for marriage and remarriage.

Support Groups

Another possibility is convening groups of people dealing with a difficult issue so they can provide emotional support for each other and supply suggestions about alternate ways to deal with mutual trials and difficulties.[11] Few people actually prepare for marriage this way and it seems unlikely that this trend will change.[12] Nonetheless, for a psychologically sophisticated group of people, a support group might work occasionally.

PREMARITAL COUNSELING

Counseling with the Couple

Premarital counseling is most effective if it occurs in a series of sessions rather than in one or two sessions or in a long marathon session. However, this is the least time-efficient method of premarital preparation for the individual couple from the counselor's point of view, because it requires an enormous investment of time if the counselor attends all sessions. So, the dilemma is whether it's better to meet with a couple over six to twelve weeks and likely help them successfully prepare for marriage, or to put less time into the preparation, even with the knowledge that it will do less good. The variety of demands on the counselor will probably determine the answer to this problem.

Group Counseling

A counselor can also convene a group of couples considering marriage and conduct a series of group counseling sessions. This will increase the pastor's efficiency and will also likely benefit the couples because the group format allows more variety in exercises, discussion, and exchange of ideas.

Lay Counseling

Another solution is to allow each couple to meet with trained lay counselors. The lay counselors might meet with the couple over the months before the marriage and continue regular meetings for about one year after the marriage. The pastor could meet with each couple occasionally over the two years surrounding the marriage and could supervise the lay counselors. Ideally, a well-functioning couple in the church might take on the ministry of preparing young couples for marriage.

SUMMARY

No congregation will have the resources or perhaps even the volume of marrying couples to use every suggestion I have made in this chapter. However, each pastor or congregation should select methods to accomplish its high-priority goals within light of its resources. In the following chapter, I will discuss ways a counselor can work with first-marrying and remarrying couples to help them prepare for marriage effectively.

CHAPTER ELEVEN

PRINCIPLES FOR PREPARING
INDIVIDUAL COUPLES FOR MARRIAGE

PREMARITAL COUNSELING IS an important service in many people's lives, possibly preventing later problems in their marriages. Of secondary importance, the counseling indicates to the couple the value the pastor or counselor places on marriage. Counseling demonstrates the expectation that marriages can work in spite of conflicts and difficulties. Finally, in his or her work with the partners, the counselor indicates the belief that they might be able to improve their relationship through counseling, which is important because it opens the door for the couple to attend marriage or family enrichment programs or even receive marital therapy should their relationship begin to deteriorate.

The *way* preparation-for-marriage sessions are conducted is almost as important as the *content* of the counseling in determining whether the couple will ever use the counseling services again. If the educational material is poorly presented, the couple will not be eager for a repeat performance. If preparation-for-marriage groups are marred by negative emotions, most couples will avoid similar groups in the future. If the sessions are unstructured, many couples conclude that counseling is a waste of time and only helps people share their ignorance with each other. The wise counselor will give considerable thought and planning to how marriage-preparation programs are conducted.

In this chapter, we will summarize principles for conducting effective counseling with individual couples to prepare them for marriage or remarriage. The following chapter will focus on principles for conducting effective preparation for marriage groups.

ATTITUDES

As a counselor, it is helpful to have *several* attitudes about preparation for marriage. These attitudes, which are discussed below, can help the couple accept what you have to offer them.

Genuineness, Empathy, and Acceptance

It goes almost without saying that the attitudes proposed by Carl Rogers as necessary and sufficient conditions for change in psychotherapy—genuineness, empathy, and acceptance—are helpful in preparation for marriage.[1] In fact, Rogers' theory of counseling is built on a model of the person that assumes relatively high psychological functioning, which is more likely to be the case in preparation for marriage than in psychotherapy (for which he proposed the theory).

Genuineness is important because partners need to trust you to accept your guidance. If your actions seem nongenuine, their trust might be eroded. This distrust, in turn, can activate suspicions of psychology and counseling. Genuineness and transparency soothe those suspicions and build trust.

Empathy is continual demonstration that you understand the person from his or her point of view. When couples seek our help, our knowledge of marriage, divorce, and remarriage often works against us, leading us to generalize and to assume that the couple seated before us is like the "typical" couple and will experience exactly what the books predict. This knowledge is helpful in allowing us to identify quickly the areas needing attention. But we must not assume that we understand any couple until they reveal themselves to us and allow us to understand their lives from their point of view.

Acceptance involves viewing the people we counsel as important, reasoning humans who are trying sincerely to make responsible decisions about marriage. It does not necessarily mean condoning all of the couple's values or actions. If the partners are theologically liberal and you are theologically conservative (or vice versa), you need not pretend that you share their theology. Rather, acceptance is affirming their good intentions.

When your values differ from theirs, you must decide whether it is vital to point out and discuss those differences. Will such a discussion help them better prepare for marriage or will it repel them? Will such a discussion assist them in their spiritual development or will it hinder them? Ultimately, you are responsible for your own behavior, not theirs. You must decide what the most effective way to share the gospel of Jesus Christ with them is likely to be. If the couple is doing something to which you cannot consent, then you are responsible for lovingly telling them, explaining your reasons, and referring them elsewhere.

Accurate Assessment

Treatment depends on an accurate assessment of the partners' needs. In my view, this extends beyond mere impressions formed during an interview with the couple. It also extends beyond the impressions you may have of the partners based on your extended contacts with them at your church or elsewhere. Those clinical and daily impressions are important, but relationships often are surprisingly different than what might be expected from knowing the partners individually.

Respect

Another important attitude is respect for the couple. Counselors expect premarital partners to be overly optimistic about their knowledge of each other and about their anticipation of the number and severity of problems they will face and how well they will cope with them. In spite of what seems to an experienced counselor as a couple's blind optimism, we must carefully avoid appearing to know more than the couple. Rather, we should affirm their sincerity, good intentions, and mature decision-making. We should seek merely to bring up information and ask questions in such a way that the couple can discover any weaknesses without feeling belittled or put down.

Expectation of Work Beyond Counseling

Another important attitude to cultivate is an expectation that the couple will continue to explore their relationship even when they are not in counseling sessions. To encourage this, you might "assign" work for the couple to perform between meetings, and then remember to inquire about the homework at the next session.

Confidence in Couples We Counsel

A final important attitude is confidence in people's ability to make responsible decisions and to change and grow even if they make mistakes. Allowing someone important to us to make mistakes is often one of the hardest things the counselor (or pastor or parent) must do. God has created us so that we are able to learn by mistakes and even to be forgiven for them. Once we have done what we believe we are led to do, we must have the courage to allow others to fail.

STRUCTURE OF COUNSELING

Stages of Counseling

As with any helping relationship, preparation for marriage will follow a set structure. I have described the progress of counseling as occurring in stages.[2] Despite my labeling these as "stages," they are not always followed sequentially; they may overlap, and they will certainly recycle over protracted counseling contacts.

Stage 1: Understanding. At the beginning, the counselor seeks to understand the person and communicate that understanding. This helps establish a working relationship between the helper and the counselee.

Stage 2: Rethinking. Building on this working relationship, the counselor helps the person rethink the issue in a way that will lead to productive action.

Stage 3: Action Planning. In this crucial step of a helping relationship, the counselor helps the person develop action plans to test his or her new understanding of the problem. The counselee places the action plans into effect to test them in his or her life outside of counseling.

Stage 4: Support. The counselor continually supports the person's attempts to change.

Stage 5: Follow-up. As well as supporting the person's action plans, the counselor also follows up on the successfulness or lack of success at changing.

Stage 6: Ending. In a final stage, the counselor and person end counseling and resume their "normal" relationship with each other, which in the event of professional counseling may involve no personal contact.

Exercising Attitudes Throughout the Stages

As counseling sessions continue through these stages, it's important to express the attitudes described earlier. In stage 1, understanding, the attitudes most exercised by the counselor are genuineness, empathy, and acceptance as we listen to people's stories and communicate to them how important we think they are. In stage 2, rethinking, we continue to use positive listening skills and attitudes, but we mainly focus on assessing the couple's likely strengths and weaknesses. We are more interested in having them discover their own weaknesses than in telling them our observations of their weaknesses. In stage 3, action planning, we need to employ flexibility in helping the people decide ways to further their knowledge of each other and to build skills for a successful marriage. This simultaneously requires that we respect the couple's good intentions and sincerity, even when we think the partners are overly optimistic or are ignoring "blind spots" in their relationship. In stages 4 and

5, support and follow-up, we expect that the partners will carry out the planned actions, and we also are mildly demanding that they continue to explore their relationship outside the counseling sessions. As we see the formal part of the preparation for marriage counseling near its conclusion (stage 6, ending), we must express our confidence that the partners will be able to live with the decisions they make.

CONCRETE ACTIONS IN COUNSELING

Active Listening

We put these attitudes into action by our behavior at each stage of the helping relationship. For example, understanding, and communicating our understanding, is characterized by active listening skills that are a part of almost every competent counselor's skills. We repeat, summarize, reflect, and paraphrase what the partners are saying so they are sure we understand them and that they understand each other. We might even ask the partners to employ active listening skills as they listen to each other.

Asking Questions

In stages 1 and 2, we try to promote discussion between partners. That means that we ask questions. Generally, partners assume they fully understand each other, so it is usually wise, when asking questions, to ask the woman how the man would answer and vice versa. I would recommend doing this about half of the time and asking the partners about themselves the remainder of the time. For example, you might say, "As you know, financial matters are often a source of discussion among most newly married couples. Sue, what is your understanding of David's role in making money and managing the family finances?" You might then follow Sue's answer with a question to David. "David, how do you think Sue feels about work and career for her? How do you understand her view about children and career?"

This type of questioning is similar to what family systems theorists call "circular questioning."[3] It not only prompts a verbalization about issues, it also tests one person's perception of the other's position and encourages resolution of discrepancies.

Such questions also put the responsibility for learning about each other clearly on the partners. Rather than have the counselor give lectures and transmit information (which can be done much more efficiently through tapes or written material), questions allow the partners to do most of the talking. This is especially true if the counselor allows the partners to discuss their differences without quickly offering his or her own authoritative answers to the questions. When the partners learn more about each other by their own discussion, the counselor is accomplishing stage 2, rethinking, with maximal effectiveness.

"Homework"

If the partners are unable to resolve their differences during the counseling session, they may come to a new realization that they have differences to resolve or aspects of their relationship to discuss more thoroughly. This discovery is naturally followed by an action plan—to discuss the matters between sessions.

Support and Follow-up

At the following counseling contact, the counselor should ask specifically how the discussions progressed and what each person learned from the discussion. This exemplifies stage 4, support, and stage 5, follow-up.

Strengths and Weaknesses

During preparation for marriage, the counselor should not focus solely on the differences between the spouses. Rather, he or she should look for opportunities for highlighting and praising the partners' accuracies in understanding each other. In marriage counseling with troubled couples who are threatening divorce, the counselor should spend at least as much time on the positive aspects of the relationship as on the negative. With the couple preparing for marriage, the counselor should emphasize the couple's strengths far more than their weaknesses.

Assessment

Assessment is the cornerstone of preparation-for-marriage counseling. In psychotherapy or marital therapy, the counselor does the assessing, using a variety of methods such as the clinical interview, assessment instruments, behavioral logs, behavioral tests, and role plays. In preparation-for-marriage counseling, the assessment is stimulated by the counselor but must be directly used by the couple. The methods are necessarily more straight-forward than are many of the methods of marital therapy, which is aimed at changing the relationship already identified as being in trouble. In contrast, preparation-for-marriage counseling is aimed at (1) increasing each partner's knowledge of himself or herself, the spouse-to-be, and the dynamics of their future rela-tionship, (2) informing the partners of pertinent information and equipping them for decision-making, and (3) providing the opportunity to develop relationship skills that may be deficient enough to endanger the future of a marriage.

I do not believe any particular inventory is a "must" for prepa-ration for marriage counseling. Rather, the inventory should fit with the values, conceptualization, and goals of the counselor. I generally use Olson, Fournier, and Druckman's PREPARE (Premarital Personal and Relationship Evaluation) Inventory, which has been found to have good reliability and validity.[4] PREPARE contains 125 items rated on 5-point scales according to the amount of agreement each partner has with the item. Answers are recorded on a specially printed computer answer sheet and are scored at the PREPARE-ENRICH computer facili-ties. Response to couples is provided on a feedback sheet, which displays each individual's scores and the amount of agreement and disagreement in each diagnostic area. The areas include re-alistic expectations, personality issues, communication, conflict resolution, financial management, leisure activities, sexual rela-tionship, children and marriage, family and friends, egalitarian roles, and religious orientation. It is possible to receive a detailed analysis of items in each area. A separate report to the counselor helps him or her determine the amount of idealistic distortion present in the relationship and the couple's areas of strength and weakness.

I also use Schaefer and Olson's Personal Assessment of Inti-macy in Relationships (PAIR) Inventory,[5] which assesses five types of intimacy as each spouse would like them to be and as each spouse perceives them actually to be. The types of inti-macy are emotional, sexual, recreational, social, and intellectual intimacy. The PAIR may be hand scored with a template available from Olson and the results are graphically displayed on a feedback sheet.

Several authors recommend other instruments. Stahmann and Hiebert[6] recommend the Taylor-Johnson Temperament Analysis,[7] a 180-item questionnaire that assesses 9 bipolar personality attributes: nervous/composed, depressive/light-hearted, active-social/quiet, expressive-responsive/inhibited, sympathetic/indifferent, subjective/objective, dominant/submissive, hostile/tolerant, and self-disciplined/impulsive. Some counselors prefer the increasingly popular Myers-Briggs Type Indicator.[8] Stahmann and Hiebert list, briefly describe, and give addresses for obtaining twelve other assessment instruments that are sometimes used in premarital counseling.[9]

I recommend that couples complete the assessment instruments prior to attending the first group or individual couple session. Instruments are scored prior to the first meeting with the couple. I limit the instruments used to two because of time and money restrictions. I usually want the couple to discuss their relationship to some degree prior to introduction of the PREPARE or PAIR profiles, but it is inefficient to hold the profiles until the end of counseling, when their results can open up many conversation topics because of the obvious lack of agreement between the partners shown graphically by the profiles.

Flexibility of Intervention

It is tempting to create standard preparation-for-marriage or remarriage programs that can be used for everyone. Yet couples differ in the areas in which they are strong or weak. Tailoring both assessment and intervention to particular couples while using standardized *modules* allows me to be efficient and still take an individualized approach with each couple.

I assess the couple in the standard areas described throughout this book: (a) individual personality and spiritual development, (b) relationship closeness, communication, conflict management, and commitment, and (c) phase of the life cycle. Then I select assessment tasks from among modules (see chapters 13 and 14). When strengths are noted, I highlight them. When deficits are noted, I question the couple about whether they want to address them. If they do, I again select an appropriate module.

Get Them to Return

One of the goals of effective preparation-for-marriage counseling should be to establish a relationship with the clients that will permit them to meet with the counselor after they have experienced married life for about six months. If they believe they have benefited from the original counseling, they will be more likely to attend subsequent sessions. Usually, though, it is necessary to tell the couple directly that one of the most effective ways to adjust to their marriage is to attend marriage enrichment sessions for newlyweds.[10]

SPECIAL CONSIDERATIONS IN COUNSELING FIRST-MARRIEDS

Adolescents

In general, partners in the first-marrying couple will be younger than in the remarrying couple, and the couples' concerns will thus be different. Many first-marrying couples will be in their late adolescence (eighteen or nineteen years old). These late adolescents will often be closely tied to their parents. Some will be marrying to try to escape the influence of their parents, but the emotional influence of their parents is still strong. This is especially true if the adolescent is trying to cut off his or her parent emotionally without resolving the individuation-separation drives of adolescence. The counselor must be careful to assess the emotional ties between adolescents and their parents, including the hidden influences.

Late adolescents are often still trying to define an identity for themselves. Their career plans are often up in the air, and the marriage will place them under financial pressure that might arrest other development. On the other hand, some adolescents are quite mature and capable of making a viable marriage work, so it is generally a mistake to condemn adolescent marriages categorically. In fact, until the last fifty years, most people were already married and had established a sizable household by the time they reached eighteen years of age.

Only recently have we conceptualized the late adolescent as immature. (Of course, immature or not, adolescents divorce at a higher rate than do people marrying when they are in their twenties or beyond.)

Young Adults

People in their early twenties have generally just freed themselves from family support. Because this young adult is breaking free of the final external ties, it is not uncommon that the family of origin will be emotionally involved in the selection of a mate. The young adult and family may be at odds about this, and the young adult's decision to differentiate from the family of origin might spark some heated discussions with parents and in-laws. In fact, one of the greatest concerns of first-marrying couples is concern over their parents' and in-laws' involvement in the marriage.

By the mid-twenties, the young adult is generally less tied to the family of origin. The first job may have become boring and the person might be considering a job change. (Most people change jobs within five years of starting their first job.) On the other hand, the time that the young adult has spent fending for himself or herself has usually built some self-confidence and established a network of close interpersonal relationships (though some people become lonely and depressed because they believe that they should be married by their mid-twenties).

The formation of a serious dating relationship or engagement is a natural outgrowth of the increasing intimacy experienced in a broad variety of relationships. Couples marrying in their mid-twenties (in our current culture) are generally considered to be "on-time" and are thus usually the most psychologically ready for marriage of any age group.

If the twenties slip away, many young adults begin to doubt their desirability and the possibility that they will ever marry. Sometimes, the previously staunch virgin will decide to experiment with premarital sex. Sometimes, confidence generated by a solidifying career path and increased interpersonal experience can offset the self-doubts created when a person begins to be "off-time" with respect to society's normal timing for a marriage. But other times, a panic of sorts sets in and the young adult tends to make a hasty decision about marriage. The counselor must be especially tuned to how precipitously the decision to marry was made.

SPECIAL CONSIDERATIONS IN
COUNSELING REMARRIEDS

Experience Influences Expectations for Remarriage

The counselor who tries to address the same topics with a remarrying couple as he or she did with a first-marrying young adult couple may be trampled in a rush for the exit. Another almost certain effect is that the couple will not attend marriage enrichment or counseling after the marriage is more mature.

Whereas parents are likely to intrude into the expectations and actual conduct of a couple's first marriage, the former spouses and children of remarrying partners have greater impact on the remarriage.

Each partner's first marriage is a source of rich experience for the couple. If the partner had a good first marriage, he or she might try to duplicate it, despite intellectual knowledge that such an occurrence would be improbable. On the other hand, the partner will try to avoid duplicating a painful first marriage. Thus, the description of the previous marriage by both spouses (and other previous marriages if the current marriage is a multiple marriage) is a necessity. From their descriptions of their first marriages, the partners will find they have firm opinions about how things should and should not be done, and they may not have discussed all of those opinions with each other.

Ongoing Struggles

The first marriage does more than just affect expectations for the second marriage. Many ongoing struggles must be dealt with. Is there continued dealing with the former spouse, the former spouse's new partner, or the new partner's ex-spouse? Are child custody disputes still raging? Are legal battles or debts from the divorce still an important part of the new relationship? Will there be continuing disagreements over parenting policies between the households in which the children will spend time? We know it's likely that many of these problems will occur, but most remarrying couples have not thought about how they will affect their remarriage. The partners simply draw on their experience in adjusting to their first marriage, when in most cases no former spouse or children were involved.

Theology of Remarriage

Another topic that will likely require discussion is the theology of remarriage. When couples decide to remarry, they may do so because they have arrived at a theological position in which they think remarriage is acceptable, or they may believe that remarriage is not theologically acceptable but they are determined to remarry anyway. The counselor may have to deal with a wide range of emotions. These might include resentment at God or the pastor. The person may show anger, fear of willful sin, depression, hopelessness, or outright belligerence.

The wide range of emotional reactions to theological interpretations of passages dealing with divorce and remarriage gives rise to a need for the counselor to help the remarrying partners decide how to respond to others in their congregation (and perhaps the pastor who agrees to remarry them).

Sexual Experiences

Statistically, remarrying couples cohabit prior to their remarriage more often than do first-marrying couples. Although we might like to believe that Christian couples never have sexual intercourse outside of the sanctity of the marriage relationship, the statistics are against that interpretation. Responses will vary with the individual counselor. Regardless of the position that is settled on, the counselor should be prepared to address this issue, which will more often arise within remarital counseling than in counseling with first-marrieds.

SUMMARY

Preparing couples for marriage requires creating a good relationship, directing careful assessment of the partners and their unique relationship, and intervening to improve the relationship when the couples desire such intervention. It also requires good counseling skills, flexibility, and a knowledge of how first-marrying versus remarrying couples behave in general. Most importantly, though, the counselor must accurately understand the particular couple he or she is currently counseling, because the most effective preparation for marriage is aimed directly at the individual couple's needs.

CHAPTER TWELVE

PRINCIPLES FOR CONDUCTING PREPARATION-FOR-MARRIAGE GROUPS

CLEARLY THE MOST EFFICIENT WAY to prepare many couples for marriage or remarriage is to use a group format.[1] Another advantage of a group format is that when several couples share their experiences with an issue, that issue seems more normal, which relieves some of the worry of any over-anxious couples. Yet another advantage of using groups is that a variety of solutions to common difficulties and issues is apparent. As a side benefit, the group also demonstrates some ineffective solutions to common problems. Often a stark comparison is apparent between how two couples deal with the same problem.

Yet, the group format also has its drawbacks. The couples may suggest a variety of *ineffective* solutions to their common problems. This makes the group leader want to hire actors to participate in the group, providing all the "right answers." A group empowers the group members and makes a leader's opinion less authoritative. Further, the group format does not allow the leader to tailor the group as closely to the members' individual circumstances since a variety of concerns might be important.

Usually, pragmatic concerns determine whether preparation-for-marriage counseling is conducted in groups or with an individual couple. If there are many couples whose circumstances warrant a group, the counselor's time is usually too limited to allow for a format of multiple counseling sessions with each couple. In this case, several guidelines can be offered.

GROUP MEMBERSHIP

Participants

The counselor needs to consider who will be allowed in the group. Will it be composed of everyone who is nearing marriage? Or will only people who are nearly the same age be included? Will couples with substantial conflict be allowed in the group, possibly creating a negative emotional climate in the group, and making it more unrewarding for all participants?

Will remarrying couples be excluded? Or, in a group of remarrying couples, will couples with children be counseled in the same group as couples without children? Will couples who are cohabiting be allowed in the same group as couples who are not?

In general, the counselor needs to know the potential couples for a group, perhaps by using a screening interview to help him or her make an informed decision about whether to include a couple in a particular group. Although screening takes time, it generally repays that investment with more pleasant groups.

Leaders

Of equal importance as the participants is the choice of a proper leader for the group. In many cases, the leader is the pastor. Ideally, the pastor should be trained in group leadership, but many pastors have learned to be excellent group leaders through their experience in administering a congregation.

Other attributes of the counselor merit discussion. Should the group leader be married? Many will argue that marriage of the leader is an absolute necessity, otherwise how can he or she know about married life? Yet the surgeon does not need to have cancer to treat the patient with cancer. Nor does a person need to be an alcoholic to counsel an alcoholic. Jesus did not have to be a sinner to counsel sinners. What is necessary is that the leader be able to understand accurately the experience of the engaged couple.

Others might argue that the *worst* initiation one might have for effective counseling is to experience whatever the clients are currently going through. Prior similar experience might prejudice the counselor, who might assume that the counselee's experience is similar to his or her own. Usually the counselor can rise above this "counter-transference," however.

In fact, I believe that it is usually helpful for the leader of a preparation-for-marriage group to be married because his or her own marriage can lend credibility to the advice being offered and provide a wealth of illustrations about difficulties and adjustments in marriage.

Another consideration is the number of leaders in the group. Should there be two or one? It might be helpful to have a male and female leader of a preparation-for-marriage group. This would allow the leader couple to demonstrate good communication techniques. Further, it would allow two people to give feedback when couples practice their own communication skills. Sometimes it is helpful for an experienced leader to colead a group with an inexperienced leader, even if the two leaders are of the same sex. This allows the newer leader to receive training "under fire" and to see how the experienced leader handles the thorny problems that often arise in leading groups.

Styles of Leadership

A variety of leadership styles exists. The autocratic leader, for example, is one who focuses the attention on himself or herself and usually lectures the couples with the primary goal of imparting information to them. Although couples may learn much from a group composed of entertaining and informative lectures, the group setting is generally not used to its maximum potential if couples do not spend substantial time trying out the things they are learning and getting some feedback on their performance.

The laid-back group facilitator usually assumes that the power of the group experience resides in the wisdom and experience of the participants. The facilitator will try simply to keep conversation going and to underscore important points made during group discussion. Undoubtedly some wise solutions to common relationship problems will be brought up by members of the preparation-for-marriage group; but there is still some need to provide information and structure, especially in groups of first-married couples.

The democratic leader usually provides structure and some information, but allows time for talk among the participants. This leader insures that no one monopolizes the conversation and that tasks are accomplished in a timely manner. Although the leader tries to keep the group balanced in terms of input from individuals, he or she does not take votes about how the group will be run.

Leadership style must remain flexible, dependent on the people involved and the overall plan of the program. For example, the pastor of a large suburban church might find that some exceptionally mature people plan to marry in June. Thinking of the future, he decides to ask several of the couples in the current group to lead future preparation-for-marriage groups, and one talented lay counselor to be largely responsible for supervising the couples as they conduct their training. The pastor chooses to colead the group with the lay counselor and to conduct a group that involves more discussion than would ordinarily occur. Because he does not want to reduce the number of lectures he has planned, he lengthens the program by two sessions. Stylistically, the pastor moves easily from autocratic lecturer to democratic director who involves others in the discussions, including the coleader. During one of the latter sessions, the pastor allows the coleader to take full responsibility for conducting the session.

Size of the Group

The counselor must make a decision about the size of the group. In some instances, such as a Roman Catholic parish, all marrying couples may be required to attend preparation-for-marriage groups. About a hundred or more couples might attend the group at any time. In such cases, there might be large sessions involving everyone, followed by small group sessions that allow for discussion.

Group *therapy* often works best if about five or six couples attend. But since preparation-for-marriage programs are usually composed of couples who do not have well-practiced problems, I prefer about eight couples. This number can practice communication with less supervision than is needed if the communication is troubled. I find three couples to be a minimum size for a group, and ten to be about the maximum that can be effectively handled by a single counselor.

Structure of the Group

Before the group is begun, the leader must decide how many sessions will be held and how long each session will be. Most effective groups have six to twelve sessions, each two to three hours long. Groups might be planned for weekly mid-week nights or Sunday afternoons.

The leader should also plan how lecture, discussion, demonstration, practice, and feedback will be combined in each session. I have given a typical plan for a session about intimacy in Table 12–1.

Developing the Program

Premarital counseling will rarely be a success if the goals of the program, and of each session, are not clearly formulated. I always write my goals, generally stating that I want the partners (1) to learn information they did not previously know, (2) to understand new concepts, (3) to apply the concepts to their own relationships, (4) to analyze their own behavior, (5) to observe and conceptualize each other's behavior, and (6) to observe and imitate behavior that enhances marital longevity and satisfaction.

Once the goals are in place, the individual sessions are planned, making sure the learning objectives are clear. Then specific exercises are planned to accomplish the objectives.

A Plan for a Typical Session
of a Marriage Preparation Group

7:00 - 7:15	Greetings, coffee & tea
7:15 - 7:20	Ice breaker
7:35 - 7:50	Talk on intimacy
7:50 - 8:00	Question and answer (Try to solicit opinions of members where appropriate)
8:00 - 8:30	Three small groups of three couples each: discussion groups to talk about three common problems in intimacy (getting more time alone and how we show intimacy to each other. Is watching television together really intimacy?). Each discussion group reports a summary of main points on a separate one of the problems.
8:30 - 8:40	Demonstration of talking about values using an "observer" couple. (Call two partners and have them discuss their views about childrearing. Co-leader and I will stand behind each partner and verbalize other important ideas and feelings.)
8:40 - 8:50	First try at practice feedback. Subgroups of two couples will discuss either (a) child-rearing attitudes, (b) working mothers, or (c) who does what around the house.
8:50 - 9:00	Debrief. What were some difficulties?
9:00 - 9:10	Second couple discusses, first couple comments
9:10 - 9:15	Summary of main points (ask people to volunteer what they learned; record their answers).
9:15 - 9:30	Refreshments

Table 12-1

Assessment

Require couples to complete assessment instruments as their ticket into the group. I justify this to the couples by saying that the devices have been found to be helpful in determining how partners might interact in marriage. I explain that we will be covering the assessment instruments during one session. Some of the instruments must be sent away for scoring, which takes considerable lead time.

Scoring fees are often cheaper when a large number of instruments are submitted together. So about three weeks before the first session, couples are required to pay a fee for this scoring, and also for reproducing material. At that time, the completed instruments are also to be submitted. Some churches may cover the cost. Others require a fee from the couples.

CONDUCTING THE GROUP

Getting Started

There is always anxiety in the first group meeting. Worrisome thoughts are common. *Should I be here? Maybe I know all this. What if the leader tries to get us not to marry each other? What if we find something horrible about each other?*

The leader can expect participants to feel threatened, and these feelings should be met head on. Acknowledge the competing fears. Explain that some people may expect that nothing will be learned from the group. Others fear that something terrible will be learned. Reassure the participants that when most people learn more about their spouses-to-be it increases their love for each other. Acknowledge that a few learn things that are threatening; but remind them it is better to have learned before marriage than afterward.

Explain the Rules

The self-disclosure exercise can be used to discuss your policy about whether people will be encouraged or coerced to participate in the group. I prefer the policy of voluntary participation in group discussion; but I ask all couples to participate in practice-communication exercises. What they discuss as couples or in groups of two or three couples is strictly voluntary, but I ask that they do participate in the discussion.

You may have other "rules," including such things as asking couples to attend all sessions and arrive on time, deciding whether to have refreshments, and making it clear that you expect couples to do "homework." You might suggest that this is not meant to be group therapy, but that undoubtedly touchy subjects will at times be broached. Couples are thus cautioned that they should reveal to the group only what they feel is appropriate and that they should treat all such revelations as confidential, only to be discussed within the group.

Survey the Goals

People come to premarital groups with a variety of goals, and it's usually helpful to make that variety explicit. Having people write down their goals before the discussion helps them formulate those goals before being influenced by the group. Then the group suggests goals, which are listed for all to see.

After the group has listed its goals, you might pass out a list of your own goals and note how similar they are to what the group hopes to achieve.

Likely Stages of Group Development

Groups generally go through predictable stages of development that have been described as forming, storming, and norming.[2] In the *forming* stage, group members get acquainted and begin to form attachments to each other. They negotiate rules and establish an emotional climate for the group. The leader helps the group form by providing a friendly and safe environment for sharing and with enough structure so that couples feel comfortable.

In the *storming* stage of the group, members have been together for a considerable time and want to modify how the sessions are run. Group members often challenge the authority of the leader during this stage. Sometimes they ask the leader politely but directly to do things differently. Or they may be more indirect in their challenges by missing sessions, violating the rules, interrupting speakers or ignoring the leader. It is important for the leader to realize that this stage is not a revolt against his or her authority, but it is a normal part of the group's establishing itself as unique. If the challenges become disruptive or combative, the leader must gently discuss them—not as challenges, but as proposals that the group be conducted differently. The main danger is that one dissatisfied individual or couple will control the group, leading it in unproductive directions. The leader should maintain a sense of nondefensiveness and a willingness to yield to the group in matters of conduct.

For example, let's suppose one couple, Will and Suzanne, are having severe conflict. They might be dissatisfied with the group's communication training because it does not meet their needs to manage their conflict. The challenge may come after the group has been working with them about their disagreement over Will's feeling that he needs more time alone and Suzanne's feeling that she needs more attention from Will. They have discussed their problem in a "goldfish bowl"—meaning they talked while everyone else looked on. Then the group members and the leader commented on the discussion. It looks as if the issue is drawing to a close and the leader suggests that they tackle a different subject when Will speaks up: "But Suzanne and I still have this disagreement. It isn't resolved."

A couple of the group members make another suggestion as to how Will might behave, but Will counters the suggestion, giving several reasons why it is not likely to work in their case.

The leader might say to the group, "Now Will and Suzanne have expressed the need for more help in resolving this particular conflict. We certainly care about them and about trying to help them with some of the difficulties they seem to be having. My question is whether we want to use the remainder of our meeting tonight in discussing this particular problem. We had planned to have some of the rest of you discuss other issues and I'm afraid we don't have the time to do that and discuss Will and Suzanne's difficulties, too. I think we will benefit from either direction you want to go; but I'll leave it up to the group about how to use the rest of our time."

The ensuing discussion helps the group build a sense of cohesion. It is important that the leader really not care which direction the group goes. He or she merely places the choices before the group.

The third stage of group development is *norming*. In this stage, the members have established themselves as a unique group, not merely a reflection of the leader, and they have established acceptable ways to accomplish their goals. Generally, the group in this stage is characterized by trust and acceptance, empathy and caring, hope, commitment to the goals of the group, intimacy, personal power (in the sense of feeling confident and free from crippling psychological difficulties), self-disclosure, appropriate confrontation, freedom to express some feelings, changed ways of viewing marriage, freedom to try new ways of behaving, and the openness to give and receive feedback from other group members.[3] Most of the work is done during the norming stage of group development. As a final part of that stage (and some describe it as a separate stage), the group must consolidate its learning and disband. The leader helps the group summarize what the members have learned. Often the leader needs to be available later to couples to discuss individually some of the issues that were raised by their group experience.

When the group members become close to each other, it is sometimes helpful to gain a sense of closure if the couples have a farewell dinner or other "commencement" event.

DEALING WITH COMMON PROBLEMS

The leader of the premarital counseling group must be adept at handling problems. Some common ones are discussed below.

The Nonparticipating Couple

Robert and Susan faithfully attend group meetings but do not participate in activities or discussions. Often the reluctant couple will participate more as they see others in the group share similar concerns and problems. But Robert and Susan have clear similarities to other group members yet they continue to be silent. The leader might speak to them in private and encourage them to share their ideas with the group.

"I know you both, and I know you have a lot to share that can help others," the leader might say.

"But we're just quiet people," says Robert.

"There's nothing wrong with being quiet; don't misunderstand me. In fact, we said at the beginning of the group that no one would have to share anything that he or she did not feel like sharing. So please don't think I'm trying to force you to talk if you don't want to. It's just that I know you both think about the issues the group has talked about the last two weeks, and I'm sure if you decide to say anything, others will respond to what you have to say and might really be helped by your insights. Just think about it, okay?"

Handling group members who try, in more or less friendly ways, to make the silent couple talk during group meetings can be more difficult. In those instances, the leader might have to affirm directly the agreement of the group about not coercing people to participate.

An instance of subtle coercion might occur if William says, "I would like to find out what everyone thinks about handling sexual feelings. How about if we all tell how we control ourselves?" If he or others then try to pressure group members to talk, the leader may want to say, "I think it is a good idea if some of you want to share on this topic. This is certainly an important one that everyone has to come to some resolution about. But I am a little uncomfortable if we set it up so that everyone *must* share. That may not be our best avenue in this case."

Later, Cheryl playfully says to Susan, "Come on, Susan. We haven't heard from you. We've all told our deepest secrets. Why don't you let us in on some of yours?"

"Gee, I can probably tell you some *real* secrets," says the group leader. "Actually, I interrupted because I wanted us to remember our agreement from the first session. We have gotten pretty close over the last few weeks and we are all curious about each other. And we want to make sure everyone is included. But let's remember that we all react differently and some of us are quieter than others. We want to respect these differences."

Differing Values

In preparation-for-marriage groups, the areas for value differences are legion: premarital sexual practices, cohabitation, financial responsibility, traditional versus egalitarian roles, childrearing attitudes, and many others.

When it comes to values, partners may disagree with each other, or with their church; couples may disagree with other couples; and couples may disagree with counselors. There are no simple answers for dealing with these conflicts. The counselor cannot always just let the couples define their own morality. Nor can the counselor always give the "Christian" position and expect couples to conform.

Let me clearly state that the correctness of particular values is not negotiated. Whether actions are right or wrong depends on their conformity to God's character (as revealed in Scripture and through the Holy Spirit) and interpreted through our reason (as guided by the Holy Spirit). Rather, what is negotiated is which values are discussed in the group, and perhaps what positions may be advocated by the counselor and group members.

The pastor or counselor who conducts premarital groups under the auspices of the church usually will take a somewhat different position regarding value differences than will the counselor who is not operating under the formal auspices of the church. This is not because morals or values somehow change depending on where one works, but because there are formal relationships that play a part in the values of counseling.

Strupp, Hadley, and Gomez-Schwartz have said that values in counseling are a product of negotiation among three agents: the counselor, the client, and society.[4] Ideally, each agent is informed by his or her relationship with God and by the guidance of God's Word. But sadly, not every counselor or client or member of society is 100 percent in tune with God's Word. It is possible for one of these agents autocratically to impose its will on counseling, demanding that the values expressed are totally in line with his or her own. But such "counseling" ceases to be counseling and becomes instruction in dogma.

When counseling is under the auspices of the church, the client and counselor have a responsibility to include the church's values, which define morality in light of Scripture and tradition, and give them the weight they deserve. This provides a strong Christian witness, which exerts its influence on counselor and client and helps shape what both will share in their sessions together.

When counseling is not under the auspices of the church, the traditional Christian values may still influence counseling, but the influence comes through the values of the individual counselor and client, rather than through the formal articulation of the church's position.

In the end, then, the values that are discussed and advocated depend on the counselor, client, and context of the counseling.

Personally, my attitude toward value differences within the group is that (a) some values are clearly better than others (because they are more in line with Scripture, reason, and tradition), but (b) each person chooses his or her own values, and (c) because I may be wrong, I should be content to state my opinions and the reasons for them and then allow people to make their own value choices. In the same way, I should be willing to listen to their reasons and evaluate my values in light of their reasoning and evidence.

I have found that an attitude such as this promotes open sharing while trying to discern what the true values really are. This attitude also avoids creating a context that I believe is unscriptural (such as saying that values are compromises, that values depend on the situation, or that no values are true).

The Conflicted Couple in Crisis

Although it is not frequent in preparation-for-marriage groups, sometimes couples begin to discuss their positions on an issue and the conflict gets out of hand. The leader will usually try to intervene to head off such a crisis before it gets so emotional that the group is disrupted.

Occasionally, though, a couple is sharply divided on an issue before the group meets, and some event in the meeting triggers a full-blown crisis between them. In those instances, the counselor must balance the needs of the group with the needs of the couple. The couple might need to continue the discussion until it is resolved. But the group might have another agenda that must be accomplished before the night is complete. The counselor, then, must decide whose needs are the most pressing. This, of course, might be done with the help of the group, asking whether group members would find it useful to work with the conflicted couple to resolve the issue.

Usually, it is more productive to deflect the couple toward resolving the conflict at a different time. If the conflict occurs during a session, you should declare a break, and quietly offer to help the conflicted couple the next day. Or you might be able to provide some immediate assistance in resolving the conflict or at least limiting the emotion.

SUMMARY

Conducting groups to prepare couples for marriage or remarriage can be efficient and rewarding both for the couples and the leader. The couples will not only learn about adjusting to marriage, they also will learn from other couples that their struggles are not unique. This can lay the foundation for positive-support networks the partners can use after the marriage. Many times, the group will continue to meet after marriage for Bible study or fellowship.

The leader usually finds group counseling especially gratifying, because positive effects beyond the improvement of marriage relationships are likely. Further, the challenges of dealing with a group of couples are different (and probably greater) than dealing with individual couples.

CHAPTER THIRTEEN

MODULES FOR
MARRIAGE PREPARATION

THIS BOOK IS BUILT ON THE ASSUMPTION that you will carefully assess couples and then apply interventions flexibly on the basis of that assessment. In this chapter and the following one I describe a "smorgasbord" of interventions, from which you can choose those that satisfy the needs of your couples and your theoretical orientation. Because remarriage often involves more adjustment than does first marriage, I have given special attention to preparing for remarriage in the following chapter.

Many of the exercises presented here and in the next chapter have been drawn from books on marriage therapy and marriage enrichment, from resources on premarriage counseling, and from my own experience.[1]

You can use any of these techniques, regardless of your theoretical orientation. Counseling techniques are fundamentally atheoretical, and have been created by theorists to help clients change the behavior, thoughts, or feelings the theorists believe to be important to the client's well-being. In almost fifteen years of supervising therapists, I have seen marital therapists use psychoanalytic techniques, psychoanalysts use behavioral techniques, Gestalt therapists use family therapy techniques, and cognitive therapists use everybody's techniques. And I have concluded that any technique can be used—regardless of the theory of the counselor—depending on how the counselor explains the technique before its use and how he or she helps the couple understand what happened after trying it.

Undoubtedly, these suggested counseling activities will be inadequate for all of your needs. However, they could form the basis for your file of interventions appropriate to your practice. The modules are organized according to the following suggested goals for the counseling session:

1. Form a good relationship.
2. Promote understanding of each partner's personalities.
3. Promote an understanding that a relationship is not just two individuals but is uniquely molded by the individuals' interaction.
4. Help the couple identify and deal with issues involving closeness and distance.
5. Help the partners communicate better over the issues they are currently involved with, and build better habits of communication with each other that will persist through the early stages of marriage.
6. Help the couple manage current conflicts and learn how to manage future conflicts productively.
7. Help the couple understand the covenant commitment upon which marriage is based, and help the partners investigate their own commitments.
8. Help the couple share their values and discuss the roles they anticipate assuming in marriage.

RELATIONSHIP FORMATION

Name Tags

The simplest way to introduce people is to have them wear name tags. As a conversation builder, participants might be asked to emboss their name tags with pictures of something important to them, such as a car, tennis racquet, tree (symbolizing outdoor recreation), and similar ideas.

Simple Introduction

Each person introduces himself or herself and says something about the relationship with his or her partner. For example, the man can describe the partners' first meeting, and the woman can describe when they decided to marry. This type of introduction can be used in counseling with individual couples as well as with groups.

Rhyming Names

In this group activity, each person introduces himself or herself with a rhyme, such as, "I'm Bob; I'm not a slob," or "I'm Sue; who are you?" or "I'm Tony; my knees are bony."

After introducing the activity, the leader begins with the person on his or her left. That person says his or her own name and the rhyme and then says the leader's name. The next person must say his or her own name and rhyme and name all others between the leader and himself or herself. This exercise allows people to learn each other's names and enjoy the humor of the rhymes. But keep in mind that some people find this threatening.

Describe Your Partner

Each person is asked to introduce his or her partner and describe one of the partner's positive attributes. The leader might begin by saying, "My partner is Kirby. She is the most enthusiastic and loving person I have ever met."

Tell a Secret on Yourself

Each person must tell their name and tell something that they think no one knows about them. This exercise is especially good for groups of couples from the same church who know each other prior to the group.

Identify Goals

People will not only accomplish more, they will usually enjoy the experience more if they are working to achieve specific goals. Each person or couple can be directed to write at least three goals to be accomplished during the preparation-for-marriage meetings. If the exercise is done in a group, the couples share their goals while the leader records them. The goals are displayed at each meeting of the group.

UNDERSTANDING INDIVIDUAL PERSONALITIES

Mini-Lecture: Understanding Personalities

The counselor or group leader might give a two-minute explanation of the importance of understanding one's own and one's partner's personality in understanding how the marriage will work. For example, he or she might describe a woman who was unconsciously battling her parents to obtain their approval, even though she had left home five years previously. This motivation continued into the first years of her marriage, inducing her to act similarly toward her new husband, always seeking to please him. At other times, it induced her to rebel against him, showing herself that she did not always have to please others to be worthwhile.

Such unconscious motivations can also affect the choice of a mate. The woman might be attracted to her mate because he exhibits the same personality characteristics as her father—or because he seems so different from her father.

Personality Assessment Instruments

Some counselors prefer to give individual personality tests during or prior to preparation-for-marriage counseling. Some such inventories can be interpreted to predict how the personalities of the individuals might mesh or clash in marriage. A variety of personality tests might be appropriate.[2]

California Q-Set

Rather than use personality assessment instruments, I prefer to use the California Q-Set.[3] This uses one hundred cards, each with a descriptive statement such as "Behaves in an ethically

consistent manner; is consistent with own personal standards"
or "Values own independence and autonomy." Each person sorts
the cards into nine piles according to how characteristic each
statement is of the person. Each pile is allowed to contain only
a given number of cards. For instance, category 9 (most characteristic) must contain only 5 cards while category 5 (neither
characteristic nor uncharacteristic) must contain 18 cards. Each
person then sorts the cards according to how characteristic each
statement is of the partner.

After the sorting is complete, partners examine the similarities and differences between the ways they perceive themselves
and their partners. This task is excellent for helping couples
discuss their views of each other's personalities and the impact
those similarities and differences in perceptions might have on
their future relationship.

Focus on Personal Strengths

As an introductory exercise with individual couples or groups,
partners can be directed to list three strengths of themselves
and their partners. The partners might discuss the strengths
with a counselor or, in a group, partners might share one of the
strengths from each category with the group.

This exercise builds an expectation that premarital counseling
will be positive, focusing on strengths rather than weaknesses
while still allowing different perceptions to be revealed.

Personal Goals

Each partner lists five personal goals he or she hopes to
accomplish over the next five years. Partners then discuss their
goals with each other. This exercise allows couples to share
their personal ambitions concerning work, personal growth, or
relationship development, and promotes intimacy.

List Our Strengths [4]

This exercise is especially effective in groups. Couples work
together to list strengths of their relationship on a single sheet of
paper. They are told that if either partner perceives a strength,
then the couple is to assume it exists. After the lists are complete, the partners share their lists with the group.

This exercise focuses couples on the strengths of their relationships while allowing partners to see when they perceive the relationship differently. When the exercise is done in a group, the group members are given a positive introduction to each other's marriages. Because the activity is done as a couple, it promotes discussion and encourages couples to view their relationships as the focal point of the premarriage counseling rather than their individual personalities.

Meeting Needs

The leader describes seven areas in which people have needs: physical, social, intellectual, emotional, career, family, and spiritual. The leader then describes how God works to meet our needs by intervening miraculously in our lives, by providing a helpmeet for us, by providing a community of believers, and by giving us talents to employ in meeting our needs. Partners are directed to write down what they think their own and their partners' main needs are in each of the seven areas. Then each individual lists what he or she can do to meet those needs. Because this assignment is time consuming and requires individuals to work separately, it is best assigned as "homework." Partners can discuss the results of their deliberations in the next meeting, or they can discuss the results between sessions.

PROMOTE KNOWLEDGE OF THE RELATIONSHIP AS UNIQUE

Mini-Lecture: The "Honeymoon" Period

The couple can be told about the "honeymoon" period of marriage, in which the partners have learned from their families of origin how to behave as spouses—or how not to behave. In the early period of marriage, the partners will begin to interact as a couple living under the same roof. They will usually experience a time when they want to please the spouse even when the spouse asks them to do something that seems inappropriate. For example, the wife might request that the husband fix breakfast, since that is the way her family did things. The husband might acquiesce early in the marriage with little discussion. This is the "honeymoon" period. However, a few months into the marriage, the husband might meet the same request with "we have to talk about this." Over time the partners usually work out the "rules" of the relationship together, which may differ from the rules of either's family of origin.

Relationship History[5]

The individuals describe their relationship history, from the time they met until the present. The counselor may then direct their attention to any of several interesting aspects of the relationship. For instance, the counselor might stress the obvious work of the hand of God in bringing the partners together and nurturing their relationship. The counselor might also stress the similarities of their relationship to the relationships of their parents, if he or she knows them. Caution is necessary, however, because the counselor's perceptions are likely to differ from the young couple's perceptions of their parents.

Graph of Emotional Closeness[6]

Each partner draws a graph of the emotional closeness he or she has felt to the partner since their meeting. Each partner then draws a graph of his or her emotional closeness toward Jesus. In both graphs, peaks and valleys are labeled so that specific events can be easily recalled. The counselor may observe that both graphs are characterized by extremes—some very high and some very low points. Usually the emotional peaks and valleys resolve over time. The counselor then notes that despite the swing in our feelings, our love for and commitment to the Lord and his love for and commitment to us are constant. So, with their marriage, they should not be discouraged if they feel that their intimacy is declining. Rather, they should remain committed and work to rebuild intimacy.

Typical Day

Each spouse is directed to jot down expectations of a typical day in married life prior to having any children. Notes should be made so that important parts of the day can be recalled. Partners then talk with each other about their expectations, perhaps discussing how long they might be married before having children, career involvement for husband or wife, division of household tasks, role of in-laws, and amount of time spent together and alone.

Next, a second typical day is described—one-half year after the last child is born. Partners again discuss questions that might arise, such as the number and spacing of children, discipline, the in-laws' role in child care, the meshing of career and childrearing for the husband and wife, the division of household tasks, and the expected life style. These discussions can be invaluable in identifying expectations. One couple, married about ten years, eventually divorced because the spouses held different expectations for their marriage, but they had never discussed those expectations until after their fifth child was born. The wife valued traditional marital roles in which she stayed home with the children. Her husband believed she was lazy for not wanting to work and irresponsible for not contributing to the family income.

CLOSENESS AND DISTANCE

Mini-Lecture: Intimacy

Schaefer and Olson identified five types of intimacy: emotional, sexual, social, recreational, and intellectual.[7] Everyone has some expectation about the ideal amount of each type of intimacy in his or her relationships. Often people state that they want perfect intimacy in every area, but in fact, people may be influenced by forces that they are not aware of. For example, a man may say he wants high amounts of emotional closeness, but when such extreme closeness occurs, he sabotages the relationship or distances himself from his wife to maintain a different amount of closeness. Individuals are invited to speculate about the forces in their families of origin that might predispose them toward more or less intimacy as an ideal.

Assessment of Intimacy

Before counseling begins, partners complete the Personal Assessment of Intimacy in Relationships (PAIR).[8] The counselor scores the inventory and provides feedback during a session by sharing a profile plotting their own and their partner's scores in each of the five types of intimacy. Similarities and differences are then discussed.

How Our Family Showed Love

Each partner writes down as many ways as he or she can recall about how members of the family of origin showed love to each other. The premise of this exercise is that we have learned much about showing love to our spouse by watching our parents and other family members. But often we are not aware that we act out the patterns learned in the family of origin.

We generally try to obey the golden rule—Do unto others as you would have them do unto you—when we show love to those we care about, including our spouses. Unfortunately, the spouse does not always perceive such demonstrations of love as we intend them. When Kirby and I were married, she told me often how much she loved me. I showed her I loved her by physical affection. It was only later that we discovered that I needed to *tell* her I loved her and she needed to *show* me that she loved me. That's the meaning of the golden rule: We want others to show love to us in a way that *we* understand it, not in the way *they* understand it. Thus, to apply the golden rule effectively, we must find out what our spouse wants and show love in that way.

How We Use Our Time

The counselor describes three types of activities: distancing, coaction, and intimacy-producing. Distancing activities, such as reading, studying, and mowing the lawn, place us out of contact with others. Coactive activities are done with others but do not produce feelings of emotional closeness. They include watching television together, playing sports or board games, working together on a common project, or talking about the events of the day. Intimacy-producing activities are those that are done together and create a feeling of emotional closeness. Intimacy-producing activities include making love, sharing dreams and plans for the future, talking about values, and reminiscing about good times.

The partners list their activities of the past week, then each partner analyzes his or her schedule to determine the balance between distancing, coactive and intimacy-producing activities. In a group, some people can share their results, giving an understanding about how each person has a different tolerance for intimacy, coaction, and distance. Couples can be told that analyzing time schedules can usually be repeated profitably after any major life change throughout the marriage.

Planning How to Use Time After Marriage

Building on an analysis of each partner's time schedule, the spouses can list together as many enjoyable intimacy-producing and coactive activities as they can recall, then note how each spouse perceives the activities. Couples are told that it is important that they enjoy the activities together and is less important whether the activities are intimacy-producing or coactive. Couples are also directed to observe that each partner may have a different desire for intimacy and that spouses do not have to meet all of their partner's intimacy needs. Many of the needs can be met through interactions with children, relatives, and friends. Further, interactions on the job and at church can meet intimacy needs.

Women used to make soap and quilts together, meeting many coactive and intimacy needs. Today, women are more isolated. Loneliness in young mothers who stay home with their children can be a major problem which the husband alone cannot fix. If a number of prospective wives in your group plan to stay home with their children, a discussion of this problem might be helpful. I don't advocate learning to make lye soap, but I do recommend women's Bible studies, craft groups, doing chores together, or getting together for activities with their children.

Women who work outside the home also often feel isolated. They may find another working colleague to share with. Recently I ventured out of my cloistered ivory tower at Virginia Commonwealth University into downtown Richmond at lunch hour. There I saw a number of women wearing stylish business suits—and jogging shoes. Walking briskly together, arms swinging in unison, they were meeting part of their intimacy and coaction needs, while simultaneously eating lunch and getting their exercise.

Fighting for Optimal Distance[9]

The partners are directed to stand facing each other about ten feet apart. They are told that people differ in how much

161

physical and emotional distance they find comfortable. They are directed to begin to talk about their needs for privacy and for intimacy. As they talk, the woman begins to walk toward the man until she is right up against him, then to back off until she is at a distance at which she feels is comfortable. The distance is measured by a tape measure. The partners return to their separation of ten feet and, as they continue their conversation about intimacy and privacy, the man repeats the exercise, moving until touching and then backing up until he feels comfortable. After measuring that distance, the partners talk about what they learned from the exercise and whether physical separation is similar to emotional separation.

Mini-Lecture: The Emotional Pursuer/Distancer Pattern

Couples are told about a pattern that occurs in many relationships when partners have had difficulties using their network of work, church, family, and friends to balance their needs for intimacy, coaction, and distance. The pattern is called the "emotional pursuer/distancer pattern."[10] It occurs when both a husband and wife have moderate needs for distance, but one person believes extreme intimacy is desirable, and also when one partner has a substantially higher need for intimacy than the other and demands that the need be primarily met by the partner.

In time, a pattern emerges. The emotional pursuer demands intimacy from the distancer. The distancer reacts to the demands by pulling away emotionally and physically. The emotional pursuer reacts to this separation by demanding still more intimacy, which perpetuates the cycle. After days or years, the emotional pursuer may decide that he or she is tired, and stops demanding intimacy. The distancer senses that he or she is no longer being pursued and initiates closeness. The pursuer, though, is still hurt and angry about the long period of perceived rejection, and he or she rejects the distancer's advances, sometimes even erecting an emotional wall between the partners and hurling insults and criticisms over it occasionally. In time, this causes the pursuer to erect his or her own wall, and the two are therefore emotionally insulated from each other.

One husband in a couple who had maintained this pattern for years actually described their relationship by saying, "Even after we have made love, I lie there with my arm around her and it feels like there's a cold steel wall between us."

We often hold the ideal that the perfect marriage is one characterized by extremely high intimacy. In that case, it would appear that the emotional distancer-pursuer pattern is primarily the fault of the emotional distancer. However, generally the emotional pursuer does not *really* want any more actual intimacy than the emotional distancer.

Couples are told that it is easier to avoid the distancer-pursuer pattern than to change it once it has a strong foothold. They are told to monitor and talk with each other about their demands for intimacy and distance, and also to balance those needs with other parts of their lives.

Building More Intimacy

Besides assessing the intimacy of a couple planning marriage, the counselor wants to help the partners build their capacity for intimacy during marriage. This is done by experiencing positive activities together, doing positive things and expressing positive feelings for each other. Here are some suggestions for intimacy-producing activities.

Caring days[11] *or love days.*[12] Each partner makes up a list of things that he or she would interpret as showing love or caring. The partner then does one or two of those things each day, and selects a special day each week to shower the partner with loving things.

Cookie jar. Three cookie jars are created: his, hers, and theirs. Each jar contains pieces of paper listing activities enjoyed by him, her, and them. Each weekend (or more often) the partners select activities from each jar and carry them out.

The "up deck"[13] *and the "fun deck."*[14] The "up deck" lists 85 activities and the "fun deck" lists 126 activities for spending positive time together. Many activities overlap. The "up deck" is aimed at promoting positive feelings in the spouse. The "fun deck" is aimed at promoting joint activities that are fun.

Share a fantasy or make up a progressive story. Partners tell stories for one minute each (strictly timed) and try to leave the main characters in cliff-hanger situations for the other to resolve.

Share silliness. Act silly together in a public place. One couple went to dinner and pretended not to understand English. Eventually the mischievous partners were taken to the kitchen to select food by pointing to it.

Love letters. Partners write a love letter to each other. The letter can be tender and serious or flowery and romantic. The counselor collects the letters in sealed, addressed, and stamped envelopes and mails them six months later. His or her involvement insures that both partners will write the letter by the date specified, and that each partner receives the letter about a half year later, when many of the couples will be experiencing difficulties adjusting to their marriage and need the reminder of the original love.

Sexuality in the Family of Origin

In a group, men are seated in an inner circle and women are seated behind their partners (facing the center of the circle) in a larger circle. Men discuss questions such as these.

1. How did my parents express affection sexually?
2. How was I told about sex by my parent?
3. In what other ways did I learn about sex?

After the discussion, partners change places and women discuss the same questions. Finally, the group is reassembled and members discuss their feelings about the exercise.[15]

In counseling with individual couples, additional questions might be discussed and more intimate questions about sexuality might be asked. For example, they might discuss what they would like the wedding night to be like.

Communicating About Sex

Couples can be paired and directed to give each other a head rub, back rub, or foot rub. First, each partner rubs the other's head without receiving any verbal or nonverbal communication. Second, the partner is allowed to communicate nonverbally. After that experience, the counselor has couples discuss the variety of nonverbal communications. For example, some couples use sighs. Others use pointing or actually moving the partner's hand in the desired way. Some simply moved their own head until it was being rubbed in a way that was pleasurable. Finally, partners give each other head, back, or foot rubs while receiving any verbal or nonverbal communication necessary.

The counselor and couple discuss how much easier it is to please the partner when there is clear communication. The counselor also points out how making love is similar to giving each other pleasure through head rubs. Making love requires verbal and nonverbal communication. Hormones and other factors affect bodily sensations. So, caresses that feel good one day may be uncomfortable or downright painful the next. Therefore, good communication is essential to a good sexual relationship. Sex is not a test of mind reading, in which one person is supposed to please the other without any communication. It is not a power struggle in which communication from the partner should be rejected. Making love is an activity that should bring pleasure and joy to both participants. To accomplish that end, communication in a noncompetitive atmosphere is vital.

Coping with Sexual Attraction to Others

Couples are told that occasionally a member of the opposite sex is physically attractive to a married person, regardless of how vibrant his or her marriage relationship is. Sexual attraction is inevitable, but marriage requires fidelity—both emotionally and physically—so the married person is wise to deal swiftly with sexual attraction to someone who is not the mate. Partners then share ways they can limit sexual attraction. In a group discussion, a variety of ways are usually described. Typically, fewer are discussed when individual couples talk.

The counselor can observe that there are two fundamental ways to limit sexual attraction to another. The person can avoid tempting situations. And the person can also psychologically distance himself or herself from the attractive person. The psychological distancing might include looking at the person as a brother or sister in Christ, keeping the friendship strictly formal, or focusing on the ongoing relationship with the marriage partner and the blessings of that relationship.

COMMUNICATION

Review of Basic Listening Skills

The counselor describes the importance of good listening, stressing only four fundamental listening skills: attending, paraphrasing, checking out, and confirmation.

Attending involves orienting the body position toward the speaker and nonverbally conveying that one is paying attention. The body position should be straight toward the speaker and the body leaning forward slightly from the waist. Eye contact should be maintained. Nonverbal assurances of listening include nodding the head and repeating important ideas made by the speaker. Dramatic failures in attending can traumatize the speaker.

When I was a fledgling counselor, not exactly brimming with confidence, I once had a client fall asleep as I was explaining a psychological test to him. He was awakened when he drooled on his own leg. I was horrified, watching a client fall asleep before my very eyes. And then drool! I'm sure there was a good reason why he fell asleep. He was probably on medication and the room was too hot and he had a test that he stayed up all night studying for and . . . (I'm certainly not threatened or defensive about it, but it didn't help that the other counselors at our agency awarded me a "prize" for Best Bedside Manner after that). Nonetheless, his nonattending behavior was tough on my ego.

Paraphrasing involves determining the content and emotional tone of the speaker's comments and describing those back to him or her. Paraphrasing may involve a summary of the feeling, such as "It sounds as if that made you furious." It may involve short summaries of the speaker's ideas and longer summaries of an entire thread of conversation as well.

Checking out has nothing to do with the grocery store. It is not leaving a hotel. Checking out is asking the speaker if you understood the gist of what he or she has just communicated. The listener might say, "You've described a lot of things all at once. Let me see if I understand what you are saying. Do you mean . . . ?"

Confirmation is a statement of the speaker that either affirms the correctness of the listener's comments or corrects some aspect that was not accurately understood.

The counselor usually presents these skills as a review of good communication, even if the couples have never learned them, because it expresses a confidence in the couples' communication skills. If a group is used, the counselor then demonstrates the skills by carrying on a short conversation with a coleader or with a member of the group. Group members then practice the skills, dividing into subgroups of two couples. One couple then carries on a conversation while the other couple observes and notes the positive communications used. (It is important to avoid criticizing negative behaviors.) Then the couples reverse roles.

Poor Communication Techniques

In my book *Marriage Counseling*[16] I provided a summary of poor communication techniques. The counselor might adapt that material into a mini-lecture about poor communication. Couples are then allowed to read and discuss the techniques and perhaps identify familiar examples of poor communication, but without using names or stories from their own relationships. Examples that are familiar to others in the group are also to be avoided, because that inevitably leads to hurt feelings.

The leader and coleader may create a short skit demonstrating poor communication. Generally, poor communication is easier to poke fun at than is good communication, as TV sitcoms always demonstrate. Making a humorous skit about poor communication will often help couples remember (and avoid) it for years.

Nonverbal Communication[17]

Couples sit facing each other. They are told to try to communicate joy, anger, fear, sadness, and love with each other by using only their eyes and no other parts of their face or bodies.

Partners may then be asked to communicate the same emotions by using only their joined hands. As a variation, one partner may be communicator and one the recipient of the communication. After all emotions are communicated, the partners switch roles.

Another variation used in a group is to hand one partner in each couple a card with an emotion written on it. At a signal, each person tries to communicate the emotion to the partner using only the face. The partner must guess the exact word written on the card. This places couples in competition with each other. The words used should be moderately familiar words, such as terror, ecstasy, fury, or anguish.

Handling Anger

Couples discuss how they behave when they are angry. Usually, each partner describes how he or she behaves rather than how the partner behaves, which helps avoid hurt feelings and criticism. The partners might then discuss their behavior as a couple, trying to discern patterns that they use when they become angry. For example, in one couple a man described how he withdrew into himself and became uncooperative when he was angry. He maintained such sulky behavior until his partner noticed and initiated a discussion by asking him directly what had made him angry. Another couple described themselves as "hot blooded," saying both partners usually jumped to conclusions and flew off the handle at the slightest provocation. After a period of shouting, they usually calmed down and made up with tears and affection.

When couples are dissatisfied with their management of feelings of anger, they might be taught Crabb's approach to managing anger.[18] He recommends five guidelines:

- Be slow to anger.
- Acknowledge when you are angry.
- Think through your goals and relabel blocked goals as desires rather than needs (because God takes care of our needs).
- Responsibly minister to your spouse.
- Express negative feelings only when doing so accomplishes a positive purpose.

PRODUCTIVE CONFLICT

What Do We Disagree About?

Couples are given a list of common topics of disagreements (see Table 13-1). Partners classify each topic on a six-point scale in terms of whether they have (1) discussed it and agree almost perfectly about it, (2) discussed it but consider it largely irrelevant to their relationship, (3) discussed it and mostly agree on the major points (but disagree about some of the specifics), (4) never discussed it, (5) discussed it and disagree about some important points, and (6) discussed it and disagree chronically and hotly about it. Issues with higher points (five or six) are likely candidates for conflict resolution difficulties.

Stuart's Powergram[19]

The top five topics (from above) are rated on a powergram, developed by Richard Stuart. Two circles are separated by some distance, which illustrates the present decision-making pattern within the couple (see Figure 13-1). On the left end of the left-hand circle, the circle is labeled "husband only" indicating that the man is thought to have full decision-making responsibility in an area. At the other end of the right circle, the circle is labeled "Wife only" indicating that the woman is perceived to have full decision-making responsibility in that area.

The partners are directed to rate independently each issue according to how they believe power "should" be distributed in their marriage. After they complete their ratings, they compare ratings. Both ratings can be put on one chart for easy comparison.

For example, Joey and Jo-Jo are about to be married. They have identified several issues that are important to them; three of them are shown in Figure 13-1. Both Joey (small letters) and Jo-Jo (capital letters) agree that decisions about how they will make love should be primarily up to Joey but should be subject to consultation with Jo-Jo. They also agree that where they will attend church will be a joint decision. They disagree, however, about whether the toilet seat should be up or down in the middle of the night. Joey thinks that decision should be his and

What We Disagree About

Instructions: Circle the number that corresponds most closely to your experience with your partner on each issue

1 = Discussed it and agree perfectly
2 = Discussed it and consider it irrelevant to our relationship
3 = Discussed it and mostly agree on major points but disagree about some parts

4 = Never discussed it
5 = Discussed it and disagree about some important points
6 = Discussed it and disagree often and heatedly

		Agree	Irrele-vant	Mostly Agree	Not Discussed	Some Disagree	Disagree Heatedly
		1	2	3	4	5	6
a.	How to spend our money	1	2	3	4	5	6
b.	How to invest or save money	1	2	3	4	5	6
c.	How much money to give to the church	1	2	3	4	5	6
d.	Amount of time spent with in-laws	1	2	3	4	5	6
e.	Where to spend vacations	1	2	3	4	5	6
f.	How many children to have	1	2	3	4	5	6
g.	How to discipline our children	1	2	3	4	5	6
h.	How much education to give our children	1	2	3	4	5	6
i.	Expectations for our children's achievement	1	2	3	4	5	6
j.	Who should be most involved in child care?	1	2	3	4	5	6
k.	Should wife work after children?	1	2	3	4	5	6
l.	Should husband work after children?	1	2	3	4	5	6
m.	How we show love for each other	1	2	3	4	5	6
n.	How we express our feelings	1	2	3	4	5	6
o.	When we should have sex	1	2	3	4	5	6
p.	How often we should have sex	1	2	3	4	5	6
q.	What we should do during sex	1	2	3	4	5	6
r.	What kind (if any) of birth control should we use?	1	2	3	4	5	6
s.	What chores should be done by each partner	1	2	3	4	5	6
t.	Should we have opposite-sex friends?	1	2	3	4	5	6
u.	What levels of friendship are acceptable with same-sex and opposite-sex friends	1	2	3	4	5	6
v.	Where will we go to church?	1	2	3	4	5	6
w.	How involved will we be in church?	1	2	3	4	5	6
x.	Do we drink alcohol or use drugs	1	2	3	4	5	6
y.	How involved will we be in outside-the-home activities?	1	2	3	4	5	6
z.	Political beliefs	1	2	3	4	5	6

Table 13-1

Stuart's Powergram

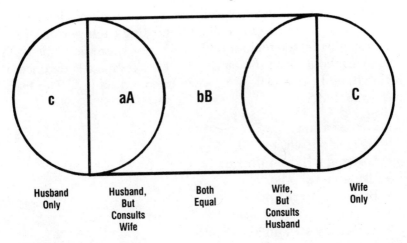

| Husband
Only | Husband,
But
Consults
Wife | Both
Equal | Wife,
But
Consults
Husband | Wife
Only |

Capital Letters - Wife (Jo-Jo)
Small Letters - Husband (Joey)

Key

aA - How we make love
bB - Where we attend church
cC - Whether the toilet seat is up or down during the night

Figure 13-1

Jo-Jo believes it should be hers. The toilet seat issue could be the underlying cause of World War III, because neither is inclined to compromise.

In using the powergram with troubled couples, Stuart recommends that the partners complete the task twice—first as they believe power is actually distributed in their relationship and second as they would like power to be distributed. I find most couples who are preparing for marriage have too little experience with each other to complete the powergram according to how power is actually distributed in their relationship. But in couples who already have significant disagreements, it is sometimes helpful for them to complete the task as recommended by Stuart.

How We Handle Conflict

Partners rate a number of unproductive techniques for resolving conflict on a four-point scale indicating each person's feelings about using the technique: (1) We never use the tactic, (2) I feel okay about using the tactic, (3) it makes me a little uncomfortable, and (4) it makes me very uncomfortable.[20] The techniques include:

- Name calling
- Raising our voices
- Leaving a fight unfinished
- Bringing up other issues
- Bringing up the past
- Crying
- Physically striking one another
- One of us leaves the scene
- Allowing the children to hear us
- Fighting in front of friends or relatives
- Keeping up the fight for a long time
- Getting into fights often; not letting things go
- One of us won't apologize
- One of us has to apologize
- Saying things to hurt one another

Tape Record an Argument

Couples may complete the above exercise and still have little idea about how they actually resolve their differences. How people perceive their conflict-management skills and how they actually argue and resolve differences sometimes bear little resemblance to each other. It is sometimes helpful for couples to pick a topic of moderate concern and actually discuss it, with other couples observing and commenting mostly on positive conflict resolution strategies if this is a group setting. You might set a rule that no negative strategy can be commented on until two positive things have been said about the couple's communication. This is not always easy. When one couple argued, the only rule was that everyone must be living at the end.

If the partners are being counseled as an individual couple, they can discuss the issue while the counselor is in the room, or the conversation can be recorded while the counselor is out of the room (or even while the counselor is in the room). The audiotape can be listened to and stopped by the counselor to point out conflict-resolution strategies that were particularly effective or ineffective. Regardless of how many negative conflict-resolution strategies the couple uses, it is good to make the positive comments outweigh the negative to reward the couple for submitting to such a threatening exercise.

Role Playing

In a group, two partners can be asked to role play an argument. After about five minutes, other couples try to identify the strategies that are productive at helping the couple reach a resolution. The leader can comment that there are *many* productive ways to resolve conflicts.

A group of four people is then given the task of coaching the couple to use *different* communication strategies to reach agreement productively. One of the four people has the "pause button"—that is, he or she is empowered to interrupt the couple's communication at any point so that the couple can "redo" what has just been said. The member who has the pause button cannot suggest new ways of communicating. Those suggestions are the province of the other three group members, who have "edit buttons." Only the most recent communication can be edited.

Training in Conflict Management

Each counselor usually develops a favorite method of helping couples resolve conflicts. Mine is the method developed by Fisher and Ury.[21] In the first step, each partner states what he or she considers to be the problem. Then, together, the couple clearly identifies the problem. The counselor tries to minimize attempts to broaden the problem or to get off task, and gently disqualifies attempts to define the problem in terms of personalities or power struggles. ("The problem is that you're an insensitive ignoramus." "Now, Sue, it probably isn't helpful to think of the problem in those terms." "She always wants her way. That is the problem." "Now, Bruce, we all want our way at

times, but we can't solve the problem if it is defined that way.")
The final statement of the problem should be clearly stated and
issue-oriented. For example, one couple defined its problem
over use of time for recreation by saying, "Our problem is to
find ways we can meet Jim's need to play competitive sports and
leave time for us to camp and travel together during the sum-
mer months."

In the second step of the method, each partner lists his or her
interests. For example, suppose Carl and Donna agree to discuss
whether to attend church at First Presbyterian Church or at
Second Lutheran Church. Carl favors the Presbyterian church
and he lists the following interests.

1. His friends attend the Presbyterian church.

2. His parents were third-generation Presbyterian and he is
afraid they will be angry if he changes churches.

3. He wants to be sure that Donna honors his opinions because he believes that the man should be "head of the house."

4. He enjoys the strong Bible teaching that the Presbyterian
church offers.

Donna lists different interests in supporting her recommenda-
tion that they attend the Lutheran church.

1. She feels comfortable with the Lutheran liturgy and wants
to maintain the feeling of stability in the time of change associated with their transition from singleness to marriage.

2. She wants to worship where spontaneity is valued, which
she believes to be the case at the local Lutheran church.

3. She wants to feel accepted, which she does at the Lutheran
church.

4. She has become good friends with the pastor and his family
and she does not want to disappoint them by changing churches.

5. She is involved in a Friday night social group that is quite
supportive of her.

The counselor quickly notes that the partners have listed arguments in support of their *positions* instead of *interests*. Then,
the counselor helps Carl and Donna turn their arguments into
interests. For Carl, the interests boil down to the following:

1. To remain in contact with his friends.

2. To avoid making his parents angry.

3. To be assured that Donna honors his opinions.
4. To have strong Bible teaching.

For Donna, her interests reduce to these:

1. To maintain a feeling of stability.
2. To have spontaneity in worship.
3. To feel accepted.
4. To avoid disappointing the pastor and his family.
5. To retain ties with the Friday night social group.

In the third step of Fisher and Ury's method, the couple is directed to come up with three different solutions that satisfy both partners' interests. If they have difficulty, they are to arrive at potential solutions that satisfy only the two primary interests of each person. Usually, the couple can think creatively and generate several potential solutions that meet both partners' interests. For example, Carl and Donna decided that they could attend the Third Evangelical Free Church, which had strong fellowship, excellent Bible teaching, acceptance, and spontaneous worship. Carl talked to his parents and received their assurance that despite his changing churches, they still loved him. Donna talked with her former pastor and his family and they assured her of their abiding love for her. They continued to attend the Friday night fellowship at Third Lutheran as a couple. A solution was worked out without either party having to sacrifice his or her basic interests, as often occurs in a "compromise solution."

COMMITMENT

Mini-Lecture: Covenant

Couples can be taught about covenant using the material I have discussed earlier in this book. Examples might be God's covenant with Abraham, and Jesus' use of the "new covenant." The counselor describes marriage as a covenantal relationship.

Discuss Commitment in Marriage

Couples are directed to discuss what commitment in marriage means to them. Topics that are raised usually include sexual fidelity, the ease of divorce in modern society, and whether commitment to the spouse is the same type as commitment to biological children. The counselor can conduct a discussion of each issue as it arises, listing main points on a note pad or on the board if the counseling occurs in a group.

Components of Commitment

Couples are shown Rusbult's equation describing commitment.[22]

Commitment = Satisfactions − Alternatives + Investments

Then they list ways to maintain or increase commitment by increasing satisfactions (through increasing benefits of marriage and decreasing costs of marriage or by lowering unrealistic expectations) or by increasing investments in the relationship. Couples might talk about the alternatives to marriage, such as attraction to others or over-involvement in work, leisure activities, or childrearing. In each case, the couples might brainstorm ways to limit the alternative attractions.

ROLES AND VALUES

Values undergird behavior, so it is imperative that couples planning marriage discuss important values on which their marriage will rest and about which disagreement is possible. Values are usually implemented by behaving in predictable ways, called roles. Commonly we hear about traditional roles and egalitarian roles, which are usually contrasted to each other. Sometimes, traditional roles are claimed as "Christian." Other people claim egalitarian roles as "Christian."

I believe the Bible does not clearly specify traditional or egalitarian role behaviors as Christian. Rather, I think that the Bible (Paul and Peter, specifically) argues that in whatever role Christians find themselves, they are to submit themselves to the other Christian in love. Whether husband or wife, parent or child, or even master or slave, the Christian is to be willing to lay aside selfish interests for the building up of the other.

Usually, couples will discuss their values and roles throughout preparation-for-marriage counseling. The topics do not need to be addressed separately, but should be covered in sections on intimacy, communication, conflict, and commitment. Many of these issues were summarized in Table 13–1.

CHAPTER FOURTEEN

MODULES FOR PREPARING
COUPLES FOR REMARRIAGE

A MAJOR POINT OF THIS BOOK has been that marriage and remarriage, while similar, are also so different that special considerations are necessary to prepare couples effectively for each. In the preceding chapter, I sketched modules for preparing couples for marriage—whether first marriage or remarriage. In this chapter, I consider additional modules that are specifically appropriate for remarriage. The counselor may select appropriate exercises to supplement those selected from the preceding chapter. The modules are again organized according to the goals the counselor may be trying to achieve.

FORMING A RELATIONSHIP WITH THE
REMARRYING COUPLE

Show You Understand

The remarrying couple usually has paradoxical feelings about marriage. On one hand, the partners expect remarriage to be similar to their first marriages. On the other hand, though, they realize that many differences exist. The counselor can disqualify himself or herself by implying either extreme—that there are few differences between first marriage and remarriage or that there are no similarities between them.

Generally, you will prove your understanding of remarriage throughout the counseling by being familiar with the special circumstances of remarriage while affirming the knowledge base of the couple about marriage. But sometimes, it is helpful to mention your credentials for counseling remarrying couples to calm any suspicions that you do not understand them.

The most effective approach is usually a matter-of-fact approach, in which you acknowledge your marital status (single, first-married, or remarried) and suggest casually that your experience working with couples is more important than your own marital status. When speaking to remarrying couples, I might say, "Actually, I find it sometimes more difficult to keep from reading my own experiences into a counseling session before a first marriage than into a second one. If I had been remarried myself, I might find myself at times trying to tell you how I handled such and such, which probably wouldn't be appropriate for your circumstances."

If a remarrying couple challenges me directly, by saying, "You can't understand us because you have never been in this situation," then I agree with them—to some extent. I might answer, "I agree wholeheartedly that I am not in your situation. Of course, the guy who got sand blown in his eyes and had to go to the doctor was probably glad the doctor was not in his situation. That's kind of a funny way of saying that it probably is more important that I have worked with remarrying couples than whether I have been one."

Structure of Counseling Sessions

Early in counseling, you will present an agenda for the remainder of the counseling contacts. One easy way to show that you understand the remarrying couple is to include in that agenda the mention of issues that are unique to the remarrying couple. That will assure most couples that you are not treating their marriage exactly like a first marriage, and it will help build their confidence in your counseling.

PROMOTING UNDERSTANDING OF
SELF AND PARTNER

Dealing with the Finality of Divorce or Death of a Spouse

One poor prognosis for successful remarriage occurs when one or both partners has not dealt with the finality of divorce or death of a spouse.[1] To help people consider this finality, have them consider the responses of a variety of people to the death or divorce: the self, the children, the parents, friends, and fellow church members.

If you are counseling one couple, allow the spouses to discuss their reactions and feelings (even if only one spouse is divorced or widowed). Then ask each divorced or widowed spouse to summarize the feelings and reactions of others to the loss. As you listen to each partner describe his or her experiences, assess whether the loss has been accepted or whether the person retains hope in ultimate reconciliation, bitterness, or extreme emotional involvement.

This exercise should be done in a group only by having couples discuss their experiences alone. After partners discuss their experiences, the group can be reconvened and a group discussion can be facilitated.

Forgiveness

Sometimes, individuals who retain deep bitterness might need prayer that God will help them forgive the former spouse. This can be especially effective in a group when others have wrestled with bitterness and can join in group prayer.

Lessons from the Previous Marriage

Each partner who has been previously married is directed to write ten lessons that were learned from that marriage. This will often give insight into some expectations partners have about the upcoming remarriage. The lessons can be discussed by each couple according to whether the partners agree that the lessons apply to their impending marriage.

KNOWLEDGE OF THE RELATIONSHIP AS UNIQUE

Relationship History

Just as with first marriages, the relationship history is a crucial part of building the idea that a relationship is more than the addition of two people. It is unique. It is especially important to have the partners describe their previous marriages (if any) as they build up to their current relationship history. I justify this request by saying, "I know it might seem painful to describe your previous marriage, but that marriage serves as a strong blueprint for what you might want to happen in your current marriage. Sometimes the path you desire runs parallel to the first marriage and at other times the path runs in exactly the opposite direction. In either case, the first marriage may exert strong influence over what you think about your coming marriage, so it is worth describing."

Mini-Lecture: Myths of Remarriage

Visher and Visher identified 10 common myths of remarriage,[2] some of which I summarized in chapter 8. These may be reviewed in a brief lecture.

Advantages and Disadvantages of Remarriage over Marriage

Couples are asked to list the advantages and disadvantages of remarriage relative to first marriage.

Similarities and Differences Between the Remarriage and the First Marriage

Each couple works together to derive a list of things that are similar and things that are different between the upcoming marriage and the first marriage. In a group, the overlap across couples usually creates a feeling that each couple is not going through a completely unique experience. After the group discussion, couples may be given a list of typical similarities and differences (see Table 14–1).

Mini-Lecture: Adjustment to Remarriage

Couples are told that adjustment to remarriage is no easier than adjustment to first marriage. In fact, because life is usually more complicated, especially if children are already involved, adjustment to remarriage can be substantially more difficult than adjustment to their first marriage. Papernow's seven stages of adjustment to remarriage, described in chapter 8 and briefly summarized here, are: fantasy, assimilation,

---

Differences Between First Marriages and Remarriages

Differences Benefiting Remarriage

Greater maturity
Know more self-motivations
Nicer to each other (because see horrors of divorce)
Children have four adults to love them instead of two
Children have two sets of parents to learn from
Faster sexual adjustment

Differences Working Against Remarriage

Divorce rate is higher in remarriage
Less courtship in remarriage
More age difference between spouses
More other differences between spouses
Children may be in different phases of the life cycle
Children are there at the time of marriage
Children require time, taking intimate time from the couple
Expectations for remarriage are less clearly defined than for first marriage
Boundaries are blurred
Schedules are more chaotic
"Ghosts" of previous spouses shape expectations
Poor conflict resolution habits may be brought to remarriage
Trust may be given only reluctantly
Lower self-esteem in remarried due to divorce or loss

Table 14-1

awareness of differences, mobilization to deal with differences, action, contact, and resolution.[3] Knowing what to expect helps remarrying couples not be fearful when the going gets rough.

Family Rituals

Remarrying couples are told that adjustment difficulties may first be confronted when family rituals conflict. Partners are directed to write independently a description of what will likely happen during each of four times: mealtime, bedtime, holidays (Christmas, Easter, birthdays), and vacations. After the descriptions are written, they are discussed. Couples note areas of agreement and disagreement and may use these issues to practice communication skills or conflict-resolution skills, since the differences are not likely to be deep-rooted relationship breakers.

CLOSENESS AND DISTANCE

Climate of Emotional Closeness

Couples are told that generally a remarrying couple holds high expectations for an intimate family life; but after being married a while, most remarrying couples describe the remarriage as significantly less close than the first marriage. There are many reasons for this. The couples are invited to brainstorm possible reasons for the decline in emotional closeness. Below are listed a few of the potential reasons that will come up in discussion or that could be introduced by the counselor.

- Children disrupt intimacy between spouses.
- Children require time that is spent in intimacy-producing activities during the first marriage.
- Although the spouse has found someone with whom to be intimate, the children do not usually share those feelings. To the contrary, to the children remarriage symbolizes the loss of hope that their parents will ever be reconciled.
- Remarrying spouses are older and often have a reduced sex drive compared with younger couples.
- Children moving into and out of the household can disrupt the intimacy within the family.

- Death of a spouse or divorce has resulted in a loss of intimacy. Widowed or divorced spouses are often reluctant to give themselves as fully to another relationship when they have experiential knowledge that it can end.

Children and Intimacy

Typically, children within the remarriage will feel less intimately tied to the family than in the first marriage. This usually bothers the parents more than the children. The parents are warned that they are likely to experience less intimacy than they desire. Two difficulties especially concern the intimacy experienced in families with children.

The naming of the stepparent is often a source of conflict. Generally, the stepparent will not be accepted immediately as a new parent. Rather, he or she must usually win the acceptance and respect of the children. The parents are directed to discuss what they wish the children to call the stepparent and then to speculate how the children might react to that name.

Parents are directed to consider the loyalty conflicts that might develop in the remarried family. They are asked to identify worst-case scenarios. In one scenario, a stepfather feels excluded from disciplining his wife's children. She says, "I don't know what to do. The kids don't really like Mark to spank them and frankly I'm a little uncertain about it, too. On the other hand, I can't seem to get the kids to obey. I feel caught in the middle." The biological parent and stepparent experience strong loyalty conflicts. Children also feel loyalty conflicts, especially if they respond more positively emotionally to the stepparent than to their biological parent.

Mini-Lecture: Raise the Drawbridge

One response of remarried parents to the perceived lack of intimacy in their remarriage is to draw the children into the family castle and raise the drawbridge. The family believes that intimacy can be created if the family members will simply pull together. Often attempts are made to cut off the other biological parent from contact with the child or severely limit the contact. The grandparents on the ex-spouse's side also might be excluded. Often, this is counterproductive in that it creates an atmosphere of ill will within the family system, and it is often especially resented by the children, who may openly or indirectly rebel.

Families are warned that the atmosphere of the household will probably feel chaotic and disjointed because the children must frequently be shuttled from household to household and perhaps from child-care facility to sporting event. Couples may brainstorm ways that they can adjust emotionally to the lack of order that is typical of many typical remarried families.

Sexual Intimacy

Couples are directed to speculate about the nature of their sexual relationship, talking with each other about how and when their love-making is likely to take place and whether the remarriage will affect it.

One danger is that spouses will compare each other to former spouses. Another difficulty is finding the time to make love. Often when complex families are formed through remarriage, spouses must cope with different circumstances than they were used to before the remarriage. Perhaps a widower with an adolescent boy marries a widow with an infant girl and a four-year-old. The widow is not used to having a child in the house who stays up as late as the parents, so she may not have yet perfected the "nooner." The widower has all but forgotten the joys of being interrupted in the middle of love-making by the crying baby, who only cries one minute before the wife's orgasm— every time. "It's uncanny. She knows. I don't think she wants us to have any more children. The kid has a great future as a censor." The cry is followed all too shortly by the four-year-old standing outside the bedroom door calling, "Mommy! Mommy! Susie's crying. Can't you hear her, Mommy?"

Other Sexual Attractions Within the Remarried Family

Couples are told to discuss the possibility of other sexual attractions within the remarried family. This might include attractions between adolescents who are from different biological parents and between parents and adolescent children. (Although no one likes to admit that possibility, incest occurs in remarried families more frequently than in biological families.)

Other aspects of sexual attraction might arise in the course of the discussion. One possibility is that competition might develop between a child and a same-sex parent for the affection of the other parent. Another topic that frequently occurs, especially in groups, is the identification of a multitude of ways that children try to interfere with the courtship of the biological parent. Couples can then discuss ways to handle the difficulties that are brought up in the discussion.

COMMUNICATION

Effects of Remarriage on the Communication Network

Couples are directed to identify all the combinations of communicators within the remarried family. The counselor should suggest missing elements after couples have named all they can think of.

- Partners with each other
- Parent-child
- Stepparent-child
- Partner-ex-spouse
- Partner's spouse-ex-spouse
- Each partner with in-laws
- Stepparent's parents-stepchildren
- Stepparent-partner's ex-spouse's parents
- Child-sibling
- Child-stepsibling
- Child-child's former friends
- Partner-spouse's friends (who knew spouse's ex)
- Partners-church members

Identifying Potential Problems in Communication

Couples discuss how communication is likely to be affected in each communication unit named above. Potential problems are noted. Later, couples discuss how the anticipated problems might be avoided or solved.

Role of the Stepparent

One special communication difficulty in remarried families with children involves the role of the stepparent in rearing the children. The couple is assigned to discuss what role the stepparent expects to have and what role the parent expects the stepparent to have. After the discussion is well under way, the counselor might mention that the children often do not accept the authority of the stepparent even when the parent and stepparent agree on the role of the stepparent. The discussion can thus be widened to include the likely responses of the children to the stepparent's attempts at discipline and at enforcing family rules.

Communication with God

The counselor might reflect on the number and magnitude of the difficulties in adjusting to remarriage, and then ask what role communication with God will play in the remarrying couple's married life. The partners are directed to discuss their potential participation in church, Bible study, fellowship groups, Sunday school, individual Bible study and Christian reading, and prayer. The place of prayer in the family should be addressed. Will prayer occur before every meal? At bedtime? At any other specified times? Will they pray together, have family devotions, or have private devotions?

CONFLICT

How We Previously Resolved Conflict

Previously married partners reflect on how they resolved (or failed to resolve) conflict in their first marriages. They describe the techniques that both they and their former spouses used and the reactions those techniques provoked. Lessons are drawn about whether the conflict-resolution strategies used in the previous marriage are appropriate for use in the remarriage. Couples are warned that the experiences in their past marriage exert a powerful influence over their behavior in the remarriage, either in trying to copy good behavior or avoid ineffective behavior. However, because relationships form their own character, the strategies that worked in a previous relationship will not necessarily be effective in the new relationship.

How We Resolve Conflict Now

By the time they are ready for marriage, the partners have undoubtedly experienced some differences that have called for resolution. On one hand, remarriages usually occur after considerably less courtship than do first marriages, which suggests that remarrying partners might have less time to discuss important differences. On the other hand, remarrying spouses have been through the adjustments of at least one marriage previously and they are more aware that resolution of differences is an inevitable part of marriage. This makes them more inclined to address some of the differences before the marriage. Unfortunately, first-marrying and remarrying couples alike marry their conception of the partner more than the actual partner. Through wishful thinking, desire to marry (which blinds people to some painful realities) and inadequate time to get to know a person, the newly married person will suffer disillusionments and violated expectations.

Nonetheless, most engaged couples have resolved conflicts. In this exercise, they are asked to describe the ways that resolution transpired. Each couple is directed to agree verbally about a time when they had a difference of opinion and then to write a description of how the conflict progressed and what kind of resolution was reached. Then the partners discuss their perceptions with each other.

Couples are told that their performance in any particular conflict is relatively meaningless in predicting the future of their relationship. Rather, their attention is directed to ineffective conflict-resolution strategies that persist across many situations until they become well rehearsed habits of communication. At the point of marriage, few couples will have such rigid communication patterns and can change their communication to make it more effective.

Potential Conflict

Couples discuss the potential future arenas of conflict and identify potential topics of conflict within each arena. Usually conflict will be possible between spouses and ex-spouses, between parents and children, between spouses, and (perhaps) between the church and the remarrying couple. Couples may role play to practice conflict-resolution skills. A method of resolving conflict should be stressed by the counselor. As I described in the previous chapter, I prefer the method developed by Fisher and Ury.

COMMITMENT

Risk Taking

Fear is often a prominent emotion in people who are remarrying. Having loved and lost previously, they fear a repeat performance. Couples are directed to discuss their fears about the upcoming marriage. They are particularly encouraged to look at a reluctance to be intimate with the spouse, a hesitancy to reveal themselves through full communication of the things that matter the most to them, and a fear of the threat of conflict to the stability of the relationship. Both the widowed and divorced person is usually fearful, but of different things for different reasons. The fears manifest themselves as disinclination to take risks. The counselor can sensitively discuss these fears, noting that for a relationship to grow, the partners must courageously take risks toward overcoming fears and hesitancies. If they do not, they may bring about the very thing they fear, a troubled marriage.

Increasing Investments

For the partners to increase their commitment, one avenue is to increase the investments in the relationship. Investments are the time, energy, and resources that are made in the relationship. One way to increase the investment in a remarriage is to have a child. Usually, having a child will help cement the relationship together[4] even though having an additional child may also place more strains on the relationship.[5] Couples are directed to discuss ways that investments in the relationship could be increased. The counselor asks the couple specifically to discuss whether they have any plans for having one or more children.

ROLES AND VALUES

Parenting Roles and Biblical Headship

Whenever children are involved in a remarriage, issues of authority of stepparents naturally occur—especially early in the marriage. The children may not accept the stepfather's leadership as "father," which in turn may disqualify him in their eyes as head of the house. When the children have lived with a single mother for several years and have become accustomed to being parented by her (and she becomes used to being the sole authority), any transfer of parenting authority to the stepfather can be a bumpy transition.

The parents must reconcile their views on biblical headship with the realities of remarried family life. Unless the stepfather adopts the children, they are legally not his responsibility. Therefore, if they do not accept his authority, are they being nonbiblical? If the partners decide they will force the headship of the stepparent on the children, are they provoking the children to anger? The spouses must discuss these issues and decide their position.

Financial Considerations

Usually, remarriage occurs later in life than does first marriage, so the partners are often in stronger financial positions than are the newly wedded first spouses. However, remarrying partners may have other financial obligations that are not experienced by the young newlyweds. For example, the remarrying father might be making regular child-care payments to a former spouse. Or the remarrying spouses may end up with three or four adolescents in college at the same time, placing a financial strain on most people. Or the children may be older than preschool age, so the mother may not feel obliged to stay at home during the day.

The family may feel financial pressure for the woman to work or the woman may simply want to work. Generally, single mothers have been working for several years prior to remarriage to support their families and they may be involved in a career pattern. The traditional values of the couple may be challenged by their circumstances.

190

Household Responsibilities

Especially if the mother is involved in a career, the role of father, mother, and children regarding housework must be decided. In families of all phases of life, the most persistent family strain is division of household labor.[6] The spouses should discuss their views about this issue. In a group, a variety of opinions will emerge and often the discussion becomes heated. The counselor should stress that there is no right way to divide household tasks, but the overarching principle should be a willingness to sacrifice one's own position in love for the other. If the partners follow that principle, they will generally be able to work out some division of labor that both can live with. If conflict persists, the couple can use Fisher and Ury's problem-solving method to attempt to resolve their differences.

SUMMARY

Most of the exercises presented here involve dealing with memories of the past marriage or with the present difficulties involving children. Giving special consideration to these factors with remarrying couples can give a couple confidence that you understand the situation at hand, and will help the partners accept you as a credible counselor.

NOTES

Chapter 1 Not Just Counseling, But *Effective* Counseling

1. D. A. Bagarozzi and P. Rauen, "Premarital Counseling: Appraisal and Status," *American Journal of Family Therapy* 9 (3) 1981:13–30; W. Elkin, "Premarital Counseling for Minors: The Los Angeles Experience," *Family Coordinator* 26 (1977):429–43; D. G. Fournier and D. H. Olson, "Programs for Premarital and Newlywed Couples," in Ronald F. Levant, ed., *Psychoeducational Approaches to Family Therapy and Counseling* (New York: Springer, 1986), 194–231.

2. Fournier and Olson, "Programs for Premarital and Newlywed Couples"; R. F. Stahmann and W. J. Hiebert, *Premarital Counseling* (Lexington, Mass.: Lexington Books, 1980); H. N. Wright, "Premarital Counseling," in D. G. Benner, ed., *Psychotherapy in Christian Perspective* (Grand Rapids, Mich.: Baker, 1987), 328–32.

3. E. L. Worthington, Jr., and G. G. Scott, "Goal Selection for Counseling with Potentially Religious Clients by Professional and Student Counselors in Explicitly Christian or Secular Settings," *Journal of Psychology and Theology* 11 (1983):318–29.

4. For example, see G. R. Birchler, R. L. Weiss, and J. P. Vincent, "Multimethod Analysis of Social Reinforcement Exchange Between Maritally Distressed and Non-Distressed Spouse and Stranger Dyads," *Journal of Personality and Social Psychology* 31 (1975):349–62;

P. Noller, *Nonverbal Communication and Marital Interaction* (Oxford, England: Pergamon Press, 1984); P. Noller, "Gender and Marital Adjustment Level Differences in Decoding Messages from Spouses and Strangers," *Journal of Personality and Social Psychology* 41 (1981):272–78; R. G. Ryder, "Husband-Wife Dyads Versus Married Strangers," *Family Process* 7 (1968):233–38; W. D. Winter, A. J. Ferreira, and N. Bowers, "Decision Making in Married and Unrelated Couples," *Family Process* 12 (1973):83–94.

5. W. R. Schumm and W. Denton, "Trends in Premarital Counseling," *Journal of Marital and Family Therapy* 5 (1979):23–32.

6. Bagarozzi and Rauen, "Premarital Counseling"; Fournier and Olson, "Programs for Premarital and Newlywed Couples"; L. L'Abate, "Skills Training Programs for Couples and Families," in A. S. Gurman and D. P. Kniskern, eds., *Handbook of Family Therapy* (New York: Brunner/Mazel, 1981), 631–61; L. L'Abate and S. McHenry, *Handbook of Marital Interventions* (New York: Grune and Stratton, 1983).

7. Reaching a different conclusion, Fournier and Olson in "Programs for Premarital and Newlywed Couples" conclude that the optimal time is between six months and one year after marriage.

8. C. A. Guldner, "The Post-Marital: An Alternate to Premarital Counseling" *Family Coordinator* 20 (1971):115–19.

9. H. J. Markman et al., "Prevention of Marital Distress," *Journal of Consulting and Clinical Psychology* 56 (1988):210–17.

10. For reviews, see L'Abate, "Skills Training Programs for Couples and Families," L'Abate and McHenry, *Handbook of Marital Interventions.*

11. E. L. Worthington, Jr., "Religious Counseling: A Review of Published Empirical Research," *Journal for Counseling and Development* 64 (1986):421–31.

12. Wright, "Premarital Counseling."

Chapter 2 The Developing Relationship

1. B. I. Murstein, *Paths to Marriage* (Beverly Hills, Calif.: Sage, 1986).

2. T. L. Huston et al., "From Courtship to Marriage: Mate Selection as an Interpersonal Process," in S. Duck and R. Gilmour, eds. *Personal Relationships 2: Developing Personal Relationships* (London: Academic Press, 1981): 53–88.

3. I. L. Reiss, "Toward a Sociology of the Heterosexual Love Relationship," *Marriage and Family Living* 22 (1960):130–45.

4. B. I. Murstein, "Stimulus-Value-Role: A Theory of Marital Choice," *Journal of Marriage and the Family* 32 (1970):465–81.

5. Murstein, *Paths to Marriage.*

6. C. S. Lewis, *The Four Loves* (New York: Harcourt Brace Jovanovich, 1960).

7. Murstein, *Paths to Marriage.*

8. R. J. Sternberg, "A Triangular Theory of Love," *Psychological Review* 93 (1986):119–35.

9. C. E. Rusbult, "A Longitudinal Test of the Investment Model: The Development (and Deterioration) of Satisfaction and Commitment in Heterosexual Involvement," *Journal of Personality and Social Psychology* 45 (1983):101–17.

10. H. N. Wright, "Premarital Counseling," in D. G. Benner, ed., *Psychotherapy in Christian Perspective* (Grand Rapids, Mich.: Baker, 1987), 328–32.

11. C. T. Hill, Z. Rubin, and L. A. Peplau, "Breakups Before Marriage: The End of 103 Affairs," *Journal of Social Issues* 32 (1976):147–68.

12. Ibid.

13. For example, Wright, "Premarital Counseling"; R. F. Stahmann and W. J. Hiebert, *Premarital Counseling* (Lexington, Mass.: Lexington Books, 1980).

14. I. Briggs-Myers and M. McCauley, *Manual: A Guide to the Development and Use of the Myers-Briggs Type Indicator* (Palo Alto, Calif.: Consulting Psychologists Press, 1985); K. Briggs and I. Myers, *Myers-Briggs Type Indicator*, Form G (Palo Alto, Calif.: Consulting Psychologists Press, 1977).

15. R. M. Taylor and L. P. Morrison, *Taylor-Johnson Temperament Analysis (T-JTA)* (Los Angeles: Psychological Publications, 1966–77).

Chapter 3 Forces That Shape Modern Marriages

1. D. Prince, *The Marriage Covenant* (Fort Lauderdale: Derek Prince Ministries, 1978).

2. E. Carter and M. McGoldrick, eds., *The Changing Family Life Cycle: A Framework for Family Therapy*, 2d ed. (Boston: Allyn and Bacon, 1989).

3. M. Zelnik, Y. J. Kim, and J. F. Kantner, "Probabilities of Intercourse and Conception Among U.S. Teenage Women," *Family Planning Perspectives* 11 (1979):177–83.

4. See E. L. Worthington, Jr., "Religious Development Across the Lifespan: Implications for Counseling and Research," *The Counseling Psychologist* 17 (1989):555–612 for a review.

5. B. I. Murstein, *Paths to Marriage* (Beverly Hills, Calif.: Sage, 1986).

6. J. Naisbitt, *Mega-Trends: Ten New Directions Transforming Our Lives* (New York: Warner Books, 1984).

7. R. T. Hare-Mustin, "The Problem of Gender in Family Therapy Theory," *Family Process* 26 (1987):15–28.

8. W. R. Mattox, Jr., "Is the 'Traditional' Family Dead?" *Family Policy* (September/October, 1988):1–5.

9. F. A. Schaeffer, *Escape from Reason* (Downers Grove, Ill.: InterVarsity Press, 1968).

10. D. G. Bromley and B. C. Busching, "Understanding the Structure of Contractual and Covenantal Social Relations: Implications for the Sociology of Religion," *Sociological Analysis* 99 (1988):15–32.

11. B. Berger and P. L. Berger, *The War Over the Family: Capturing the Middle Ground* (Garden City, N. Y.: Anchor Press/Doubleday, 1984).

Chapter 4 A Psychology of Marriage

1. This theory of marriage is described in E. L. Worthington, Jr., *Marriage Counseling: A Christian Approach to Counseling Couples* (Downers Grove, Ill.: InterVarsity Press, 1989).

2. I have summarized this in detail in Worthington, *Marriage Counseling;* see also P. Steinglass, "The Conceptualization of Marriage from a Systems Theory Perspective," in T. J. Paolino and B. S. McCrady, eds., *Marriage and Marital Therapy* (New York: Brunner/ Mazel, 1978):298–365.

3. J. Haley, *Strategies of Psychotherapy* (New York: Grune and Stratton, 1963); P. Watzlawick, J. B. Bavelas, and D. Jackson, *Pragmatics of Human Communication* (New York: Norton, 1967).

4. M. T. Schaefer and D. H. Olson, "Assessing Intimacy: The PAIR Inventory," *Journal of Marital and Family Therapy* 7 (1981):47–60.

5. R. Fisher and W. Ury, *Getting to Yes: Negotiating Agreement Without Giving In* (New York: Penguin Books, 1981).

6. R. M. Cate, S. A. Lloyd, and E. Long, "The Role of Rewards and Fairness in Developing Premarital Relationships," *Journal of Marriage and the Family* 50 (1988):443–52.

7. R. A. Lewis, "A Developmental Framework for the Analysis of Premarital Dyadic Formation," *Family Process* 11 (1972):17–48.

8. A. J. Cherlin, *Marriage, Divorce, Remarriage* (Cambridge, Mass.: Harvard University Press, 1981).

Chapter 5 Can Christians Accept Divorced People?

1. C. J. Barber, "Marriage, Divorce, and Remarriage," *Journal of Psychology and Theology* 12 (1984):170–77.

2. J. C. Laney, *The Divorce Myth* (Minneapolis: Bethany, 1981).

3. See J. E. Adams, *Marriage, Divorce and Remarriage in the Bible* (Grand Rapids, Mich.: Baker, 1980); G. W. Bromiley, *God and Marriage* (Grand Rapids, Mich.: Eerdmans, 1980); G. Duty, *Divorce and Remarriage* (Minneapolis: Bethany, 1977); S. A. Ellisen, *Divorce and Remarriage in the Church* (Grand Rapids, Mich.: Zondervan, 1980); M. Kysar and R. Kysar, *The Asundered: Biblical Teachings on Divorce and Remarriage* (Atlanta, John Knox, 1978); J. F. MacArthur, Jr., *The Family* (Chicago: Moody, 1982); L. O. Richards, *Remarriage: Healing Gift from God* (Waco, Tex.: Word, 1981).

4. Ellisen, *Divorce and Remarriage in the Church.*

5. K. T. Kelly, *Divorce and Second Marriage: Facing the Challenge* (New York: Seabury, 1983); J. J. Young, *Divorce Ministry and the Marriage Tribunal* (New York: Paulist, 1982); J. P. Zwack, *Annulment: Your Chance to Remarry Within the Catholic Church* (New York: Harper and Row, 1983).

6. Barber, "Marriage, Divorce, and Remarriage."

Chapter 6 Effects of Widowhood and Divorce

1. T. H. Holmes and R. H. Rahe, "The Social Readjustment Rating Scale," *Journal of Psychosomatic Research* 11 (1967):213–18.

2. E. L. Worthington, Jr., *Marriage Counseling: A Christian Approach to Counseling Couples* (Downers Grove, Ill.: InterVarsity Press, 1989).

3. E. M. Hetherington, M. Stanley-Hagan, and E. R. Anderson, "Marital Transitions: A Child's Perspective," *American Psychologist* 44 (1989):303–12.

4. J. P. Hill, "The Family," in M. Johnson, ed., *Toward Adolescence: The Middle School Years*, (Chicago: University of Chicago Press, 1980): 32–55; J. P. Hill et al., "Pubertal Status and Parent-Child Relations in Families of Seventh-Grade Boys," *Journal of*

Early Adolescence 5 (1985):31–44; J. P. Hill et al., "Menarcheal Status and Parent-Child Relations in Families of Seventh-Grade Girls," *Journal of Youth and Adolescence* 14 (1985):301–16.

5. G. Levinger, "Marital Cohesiveness and Dissolution: An Integrative Review," *Journal of Marriage and the Family* 27 (1965):19–28.

6. R. A. Lewis and G. B. Spanier, "Theorizing About the Quality and Stability of Marriage," in W. R. Burr et al., eds., *Contemporary Theories About the Family* (New York: Free Press, 1979): 268–94.

7. Lewis and Spanier, "Theorizing"; S. J. Price and P. C. McKenry, *Divorce* (Newbury Park, Calif.: Sage, 1988).

8. Price and McKenry, *Divorce.*

9. R. R. Bell, *Marriage and Family Interactions* (Homewood: Ill.: Dorsey, 1979); G. R. Leslie, *The Family in Social Context* (New York: Oxford University Press, 1982).

10. Price and McKenry, *Divorce.*

11. R. J. Galligan and S. J. Bahr, "Economic Well-Being and Marital Stability: Implications for Income Maintenance Programs," *Journal of Marriage and the Family* 40 (1978):283–90; S. J. South and G. Spitzer, "Determinants of Divorce Over the Marital Life Course," *American Sociological Review* 51 (1986):583–90.

12. South and Spitzer, "Determinants of Divorce."

13. Price and McKenry, *Divorce.*

14. E. L. Worthington, Jr., *Marriage Counseling: A Christian Approach to Counseling Couples* (Downers Grove, Ill.:InterVarsity Press, 1989).

15. B. S. Strong and C. DeVault, *The Marriage and Family Experience* (St. Paul, Minn.: West, 1986).

16. Price and McKenry, *Divorce.*

17. Lewis and Spanier, "Theorizing."

18. A. Thornton, "Marital Instability Differences and Interactions: Insights from Multivariate Contingency Tables," *Sociology and Social Research* 62 (1978):572–95; A. Thornton, "Changing Attitudes Toward Separation and Divorce: Causes and Consequences," *American Journal of Sociology* 90 (1985):856–972; J. J. Young, "The Divorced Catholics Movement," *Journal of Divorce* 2 (1978):83–97.

19. Thornton, "Marital Instability Differences."

20. J. R. Eshleman, *The Family: An Introduction* (Boston: Allyn and Bacon, 1985).

21. S. M. Bishop and G. M. Ingersoll, "Effects of Marital Conflict and Family Structure on the Self-Concepts of Pre- and Early Adolescents," *Journal of Youth and Adolescence* 18 (1989):25–38; A. H. Fishel, "Children's Adjustment in Divorced Families," *Youth*

and Society 19 (1987):173–96; Hetherington et al., "Marital Transitions"; J. B. Kelly, "Longer-Term Adjustment in Children of Divorce: Converging Findings and Implications for Practice," *Journal of Family Psychology* 2 (1988):119–40.

22. J. Wallerstein and S. Blakeslee, *Second Chances: Men, Women, and Children a Decade After Divorce* (New York: Ticknor and Fields, 1989).

23. For a review, see Kelly, "Longer-Term Adjustment in Children of Divorce."

24. South and Spitzer, "Determinants of Divorce."

25. For a review of research, see E. L. Worthington, Jr., *Counseling for Unplanned Pregnancy and Infertility* (Waco, Tex.: Word, 1987).

26. See G. H. Brody, E. Neubaum, and R. Forehand, "Serial Marriage: A Heuristic Analysis of an Emerging Family Form," *Psychological Bulletin* 103 (1988):211–22. This research indicates divorce is more likely and duration of each marriage is shorter with each subsequent marriage.

27. Lewis and Spanier, "Theorizing."

28. Price and McKenry, *Divorce.*

29. F. Pittman, *Private Lies: Infidelity and the Betrayal of Intimacy* (New York: W. W. Norton, 1989).

30. Price and McKenry, *Divorce.*

31. B. L. Bloom, R. L. Niles, and A. M. Tatcher, "Sources of Marital Dissatisfaction Among Newly Separated Persons," *Journal of Family Issues* 6 (1985):359–73; G. C. Kitson, "Marital Discord and Marital Separation: A County Survey," *Journal of Marriage and the Family* 47 (1985):693–700; M. Thurnker et al., "Sociodemographics: Perspectives on Reasons for Divorce," *Journal of Divorce* 6 (1983):25–35.

32. Price and McKenry, *Divorce.*

33. P. Bohannan, "The Six Stations of Divorce," in P. Bohannan, ed. *Divorce and After* (Garden City, N.Y.: Doubleday, 1970); D. J. Froiland and T. L. Hozman, "Counseling for Constructive Divorce," *Personnel and Guidance Journal* 55 (1977):525–29; S. Kessler, *The American Way of Divorce: Prescriptions for Change* (Chicago: Nelson Hall, 1975); S. Kraus, "The Crisis of Divorce: Growth Promoting or Pathogenic," *Journal of Divorce* 2 (1979):107–19; S. Price-Bonham and J. O. Balswick, "The Noninstitutions: Divorce, Desertion, and Remarriage," *Journal of Marriage and the Family* 42 (1980):225–38; C. J. Salts, "Divorce Process: Integrating Theory," *Journal of Divorce* 2(1979):233–40; R. S. Wiseman, "Crisis Theory and the Process of Divorce," *Social Casework* 56 (1975):205–12.

34. Price and McKenry, *Divorce.*

35. For a review see Price and McKenry, *Divorce.*

36. S. L. Albrecht, "Reactions and Adjustments to Divorce: Differences in the Experiences of Males and Females," *Family Relations* 29 (1980):59–69.

37. L. I. Pearlin and C. Schooler, "The Structure of Coping," *Journal of Health and Social Behavior* 19 (1978):2–21.

38. For a review, see Price and McKenry, *Divorce.*

39. Price and McKenry, *Divorce.*

40. For a review, see Kelly, "Longer-Term Adjustment in Children of Divorce."

41. M. E. Bowman and C. R. Ahrons, "Impact of Legal Custody Status on Fathers' Parenting Postdivorce," *Journal of Marriage and the Family* 47 (1985):481–88; W. S. Coysh et al., "Parental Postdivorce Adjustment in Joint and Sole Physical Custody Families," *Journal of Family Issues* 10 (1989):52–71; E. M. Hetherington, M. Cox, and R. Cox, "Effects of Divorce on Parents and Children," in M. Lamb, ed. *Nontraditional Families* (Hillsdale, N. J.: Lawrence Erlbaum, 1982):233–88; L. I. Pearlin and J. L. Johnson, "Marital Status, Life-Strains and Depression," *American Sociological Review* 42 (1977):704–15; G. B. Spanier and L. Thompson, *Parting: The Aftermath of Separation and Divorce* (Beverly Hills, Calif.: Sage, 1984); J. Wallerstein and J. B. Kelly, *Surviving the Breakup: How Children and Parents Cope with Divorce* (New York: Basic Books, 1982).

42. For one review of research comparing divorce and widowhood, see G. C. Kitson et al., "Adjustment to Widowhood and Divorce: A Review," *Journal of Family Issues* 10 (1989):5–32.

43. B. L. Bloom, S. J. Asher, and S. W. White, "Disruption as a Stressor: A Review and Analysis," *Psychological Bulletin* 85 (1978):867–94; Kitson et al., "Adjustment to Widowhood and Divorce"; A. R. Somers, "Marital Status, Health, and Use of Health Services," *Journal of the American Medical Association* 241 (1979):1818–22; L. M. Verbrugge, "Marital Status and Health," *Journal of Marriage and the Family* 41 (1979):267–85.

44. J. Farnsworth, M. A. Pett, and D. A. Lund, "Predictors of Loss Management and Well-Being in Later Life Widowhood and Divorce," *Journal of Family Issues* 10 (1989):102–21; W. R. Gove and H. C. Shin, "The Psychological Well-Being of Divorced and Widowed Men and Women: An Empirical Analysis," *Journal of Family Issues* 10 (1989):122–44; Kitson et al., "Adjustment to Widowhood and Divorce."

45. For a review, see Kitson et al., "Adjustment to Widowhood and Divorce."

46. L. A. Morgan, "Economic Well-Being Following Marital Termination: A Comparison of Widowed and Divorced Women," *Journal of Family Issues* 10 (1989):86–101.

47. Farnsworth, Pett, and Lund, "Predictors of Loss Management."

48. P. J. Clayton, "The Sequelae and Nonsequelae of Conjugal Bereavement," *American Journal of Psychiatry* 136 (1979):1530–34; Coysh et al., "Parental Postdivorce Adjustment in Joint and Sole Physical Custody Families"; G. C. Kitson, A. V. Graham, and D. D. Schmidt, "Troubled Marriages and Divorce: A Prospective Suburban Study," *Journal of Family Practice* 17 (1983):249–58.

49. C. M. Parkes and R. S. Weiss, *Recovery from Bereavement* (New York: Basic Books, 1983).

50. S. Zisook and S. R. Shuchter, "The First Four Years of Widowhood," *Psychiatric Annals* 16 (1986):289–94.

51. J. S. Wallerstein, "Women after Divorce: Preliminary Report from a Ten-Year Follow-up," *American Journal of Orthopsychiatry* 56 (1986):65–77.

52. R. W. Greene and S. Feld, "Social Support Coverage and the Well-Being of Elderly Widows and Married Women," *Journal of Family Issues* 10 (1989):33–51.

Chapter 7 A Theology of Remarriage

1. D. H. Small, *The Right to Remarry* (Old Tappan, N.J.: Revell, 1975).

2. R. J. Plekker, *Divorce and the Christian: What the Bible Teaches* (Wheaton, Ill.: Tyndale, 1980).

3. J. E. Adams, *Marriage, Divorce and Remarriage in the Bible* (Grand Rapids, Mich.: Baker, 1980).

4. H. Virkler, "Divorce, Remarriage and the Christian Counselor," a paper presented at the meeting of the Christian Association for Psychological Studies, Chicago (April 1978).

5. S. A. Ellisen, *Divorce and Remarriage in the Church* (Grand Rapids, Mich.: Zondervan, 1980).

6. G. R. Collins, *Christian Counseling*, rev. ed. (Dallas: Word, 1988).

Chapter 8 The Dynamics of Remarriage

1. P. C. Glock, "Marriage, Divorce, and Living Arrangements: Prospective Changes," *Journal of Family Issues* 5 (1984):7–26.

2. G. H. Brody, E. Neubaum, and R. Forehand, "Serial Marriage: A Heuristic Analysis of an Emerging Family Form," *Psychological Bulletin* 103 (1988); A. J. Cherlin, *Marriage, Divorce, Remarriage* (Cambridge, Mass.: Harvard University Press, 1981).

3. E. B. Visher and J. S. Visher, *Old Loyalties, New Ties: Therapeutic Strategies with Stepfamilies* (New York: Brunner/Mazel, 1988).

4. W. Lederer and D. D. Jackson, *Mirages of Marriage* (New York: W. W. Norton, 1968).

5. F. F. Furstenberg and G. B. Spanier, *Recyclying the Family* (Beverly Hills, Calif.: Sage, 1984).

6. C. R. Ahrons and L. Wallisch, "Parenting in the Binuclear Family: Relationships Between Biological and Stepparents"; K. Pasley and M. Ihinger-Tallman, ed. *Remarriage and Stepparenting: Current Research and Theory* (New York: Guilford, 1987); W. G. Clingempeel, E. Brand, and R. Ievoli,"Stepparent-Stepchild Relationships in Stepmother and Stepfather Families: A Multimethod Study," *Family Relations* 33 (1984):465–73.

7. Clingempeel, Brand, and Ievoli, "Stepparent-Stepchild Relationships."

8. Visher and Visher, *Old Loyalties.*

9. L. H. Ganong and M. Coleman, "The Effects of Remarriage on Children: A Review of the Empirical Literature," *Family Relations* 33 (1984):389–408.

10. Visher and Visher, *Old Loyalties.*

11. Ibid.

12. M. Ihinger-Tallman and K. Pasley, *Remarriage* (Newbury Park, Calif.: Sage, 1987).

13. L. K. White and A. Booth, "The Quality and Stability of Remarriages: The Role of Stepchildren," *American Sociological Review* 50 (1985):689–98.

14. Ihinger-Tallman and Pasley, *Remarriage;* T. W. Roberts and S. J. Price,"Instant Families: Divorced Mothers Marry Never-Married Men," *Journal of Divorce* 11 (1987):71–93.

15. L. H. Ganong and M. Coleman, "A Comparison of Clinical and Empirical Literature on Children in Stepfamilies," *Journal of Marriage and the Family* 48 (1986):309–18; L. H. Ganong and M. Coleman, "Preparing for Remarriage: Anticipating the Issues, Seeking Solutions," *Family Relations* 38 (1988):28–33.

16. C. Hobart, "Parent-Child Relations in Remarried Families," *Journal of Family Issues* 8 (1987):259–77.

17. E. M. Hetherington, M. Cox, and R. Cox, "Long-Term Effects of Divorce and Remarriage on the Adjustment of Children,"

Journal of the American Academy of Child Psychiatry 24 (1985): 518–30.

18. A. DeMaris, "A Comparison of Remarriages with First Marriages on Satisfaction in Marriage and its Relationship to Prior Cohabitation," *Family Relations* 33 (1984):443–49; L. Duberman, *The Reconstituted Family: A Study of Remarried Couples and Their Children* (Chicago: Nelson-Hall, 1975); N. D. Glenn and C. N. Weaver, "The Marital Happiness of Remarried Divorced Persons," *Journal of Marriage and the Family* 39 (1977):331–37; J. R. Pink and K. S. Wampler, "Problem Areas in Stepfamilies: Cohesion, Adaptability, and the Stepfather-Adolescent Relationship," *Family Relations* 34 (1985):327–35; K. S. Renee, "Health and Marital Experience in an Urban Population," *Journal of Marriage and the Family* 33 (1971):338–50; H. R. Weingarten, "Remarriage and Well-Being: National Survey Evidence of Social and Psychological Effects," *Journal of Family Issues* 1 (1980):533–59; White and Booth, "The Quality and Stability of Remarriages."

19. For a review see Brody, Neubaum, and Forehand, "Serial Marriage."

20. B. E. Aguirre and W. C. Parr, "Husband's Marriage Order and the Stability of First and Second Marriages of White and Black Women," *Journal of Marriage and the Family* 44 (1982):605–20; G. Dean and D. T. Gurak, "Marital Homogamy the Second Time Around," *Journal of Marriage and the Family* 40 (1978):559–69.

21. Dean and Gurak, "Marital Homogamy."

22. Visher and Visher, *Old Loyalties.*

23. E. B. Visher and J. S. Visher, *Stepfamilies: A Guide to Working with Stepparents and Stepchildren* (New York: Brunner/Mazel, 1979).

24. K. Walker and L. Messinger, "Remarriage after Divorce: Dissolution and Reconstruction of Family Boundaries," *Family Process* 18 (1979):185–92.

25. C. Hobart, "The Family System in Remarriage: An Exploratory Study," *Journal of Marriage and the Family* 50 (1988):649–61.

26. B. Schlesinger, "Remarriage—An Inventory of Findings," *Family Coordinator* 17 (1968):248–60.

27. J. H. Larson and S. M. Allgood, "A Comparison of Intimacy in First-Married and Remarried Couples," *Journal of Family Issues* 8 (1987):319–31.

28. C. Broderick, *Couples* (New York: Simon and Schuster, 1979); J. H. Larson, J. Anderson, and A. Morgan, *Effective Stepparenting* (New York: Family Service Association of America, 1984); B. Schlesinger, "Remarriage as Family Reorganization for

Divorced Persons—A Canadian Study," *Journal of Comparative Family Studies* 1 (1970):101–18.

29. Cherlin, *Marriage, Divorce, Remarriage.*

30. Ibid.

31. L. Messinger, "Remarriage Between Divorced People with Children from Previous Marriages: A Proposal for Preparation for Remarriage," *Journal of Marriage and Family Counseling* 2 (1976):193–200.

32. Larson and Allgood, "A Comparison of Intimacy."

33. C. W. Peek et al., "Patterns of Functioning in Families of Remarried and First-Married Couples," *Journal of Marriage and the Family* 50 (1988):699–708.

34. M. M. Hunt, *The World of the Formerly Married* (New York: McGraw-Hill, 1966).

35. Hunt, *Formerly Married;* M. B. Isaacs and G. H. Leon, "Remarriage and its Alternatives Following Divorce: Mother and Child Adjustment," *Journal of Marital and Family Therapy* 14 (1988):163–73; K. M. O'Flaherty and L. W. Eels, "Courtship Behavior of the Remarried," *Journal of Marriage and the Family* 50 (1988):499–506.

36. A. B. Hollingshead, "Marital Status and Wedding Behavior," *Marriage and Family Living* 14 (1952):308–11.

37. J. Bernard, *Remarriage: A Study of Marriage* (New York: Dryden, 1956); E. Fox, *Marriage Go Round* (Lanham, Mass.: University Press of America, 1983); E. E. LeMasters, "The Courtship of Older Persons," *Midwest Sociologist* 20 (1957):8–11.

38. Compare with J. H. Peters, "Comparison of Mate Selection and Marriage in the First and Second Marriage in a Selected Sample of the Remarried," *Journal of Comparative Family Studies* 7 (1976):483–91.

39. For a fuller account of these phases, see F. H. Brown, "The Postdivorce Family," in E. Carter and M. McGoldrick, eds. *The Changing Family Life Cycle: A Framework for Family Therapy,* 2d ed. (Boston: Allyn and Bacon, 1989), 371–98.

40. P. C. Glick, "Remarriage: Some Recent Changes and Variations," *Journal of Family Issues* 1 (1980):455–78.

41. Isaacs and Leon, "Remarriage and its Alternatives."

42. O'Flaherty and Eels, "Courtship Behavior of the Remarried."

43. P. Papernow, "The Stepfamily Cycle: An Experiential Model of Stepfamily Development," *Family Relations* 33 (1984):355–63.

44. B. Carter and M. McGoldrick, "Overview: The Changing Family Life Cycle—A Framework for Family Therapy," in Carter

and McGoldrick, eds., *The Changing Family Life Cycle,* 3–28; and M. McGoldrick and B. Carter, "Forming a Remarried Family," in Carter and McGoldrick, eds., *The Changing Family Life Cycle,* 399–429.

45. E. M. Hetherington, M. Stanley-Hagan, and E. R. Anderson, "Marital Transitions: A Child's Perspective," *American Psychologist* 44 (1989); McGoldrick and Carter, "Forming a Remarried Family."

46. A. S. Dahl, K. M. Cowgill, and E. Asmundsson, "Life in Remarriage Families," *Social Work* 32 (1987):40–44.

47. McGoldrick and Carter, "Forming a Remarried Family."

Chapter 9 Difficulties in Adjusting to Remarriage

1. J. B. Kelly, "Longer-Term Adjustment in Children of Divorce: Converging Findings and Implications for Practice," *Journal of Family Psychology* 2 (1988).

2. Kelly, "Longer-Term Adjustment in Children of Divorce."

3. E. B. Visher and J. S. Visher, *Old Loyalties, New Ties: Therapeutic Strategies with Stepfamilies* (New York: Brunner/Mazel, 1988).

4. Visher and Visher, *Old Loyalties.*

5. Ibid.

6. Ibid.

7. Ibid.

8. P. Bohannan and H. Yahraes, "Stepfathers as Parents," in E. Corfman, ed. *Families Today: A Research Sampler on Families and Children,* National Institute of Mental Health Science Monograph (Washington, D.C.: Government Printing Office, 1979):347–362; H. R. Weingarten, "Remarriage and Well-Being: National Survey Evidence of Social and Psychological Effects," *Journal of Family Issues* 1 (1980)."

9. T. O. Anderson, "The Effect of Stepfather/Stepchild Interaction on Stepfamily Adjustment," *Dissertation Abstracts International* 43 (1982):1306A.

10. W. S. Clingempeel, E. Brand, and R. Ievoli, "Stepparent-Stepchild Relationships in Stepmother and Stepfather Families: A Multi-Method Study," *Family Relations* 33 (1984):465–73; J. W. Santrock et al., "Children's and Parents' Observed Social Behavior in Stepfather Families," *Child Development* 53 (1982):472–80.

11. M. I. Hafkin, "Association Factors for Stepfathers' Integration Within the Blended Family," *Dissertation Abstracts International* 42 (1981):4578B.

12. Clingempeel, Brand, and Ievoli, "Stepparent-Stepchild Relationships"; E. Ferri, *Stepchildren: A National Study* (Windsor, England: NFER-Nelson, 1984).

13. J. Nadler, "The Psychological Stress of the Stepmother," *Dissertation Abstracts International* 37 (1976):5367B.

14. C. E. Rusbult, "A Longitudinal Test of the Investment Model: The Development (and Deterioration) of Satisfaction and Commitment in Heterosexual Involvement," *Journal of Personality and Social Psychology* 45 (1983): 101–17.

15. T. W. Roberts and S. J. Price, "Instant Families: Divorced Mothers Marry Never-Married Men," *Journal of Divorce* 11 (1987).

Chapter 10 Programs to Prepare Couples for Marriage

1. D. G. Fournier and D. H. Olson, "Programs for Premarital and Newlywed Couples," in Ronald F. Levant, ed., *Psychoeducational Approaches to Family Therapy and Counseling* (New York: Springer, 1986).

2. I am relying on my memory for a summary of the sermon, so I apologize to Pastor McMurry if I have mutilated his ideas through my faulty memory.

3. J. R. W. Stott, *Marriage and Divorce* (Downers Grove, Ill.: InterVarsity Press, 1984).

4. Many excellent lay counseling programs exist, built on writings of counselors such as J. E. Adams, *The Christian Counselor's Manual* (Nutley, N.J.: Presbyterian and Reformed, 1973); G. R. Collins, *How to Be a People Helper* (Ventura, Calif.: Regal Books, 1976); G. R. Collins, *Innovative Approaches to Counseling* (Waco, Tex.: Word, 1986):71–88; L. Crabb, Jr., *Effective Biblical Counseling* (Grand Rapids, Mich.: Zondervan, 1977); S. Y. Tan, ed. "Lay Christian Counseling," *Journal of Psychology and Christianity* 6, no. 2 (1987):1–84; P. Welter, *How to Help a Friend*, rev. ed. (Wheaton, Ill.: Tyndale House, 1990); E. L. Worthington, Jr., *When Someone Asks for Help: A Practical Guide for Counseling* (Downers Grove, Ill.: InterVarsity Press, 1982); E. L. Worthington, Jr., *How to Help the Hurting: When Friends Face Problems with Self-Esteem, Self-Control, Fear, Depression, Loneliness* (Downer's Grove, Ill.: InterVarsity Press, 1985).

5. R. F. Stahmann and W. J. Hiebert, *Premarital Counseling* (Lexington, Mass.: Lexington Books, 1980); H. N. Wright, "Premarital Counseling," in D. G. Benner, ed., *Psychotherapy in Christian Perspective* (Grand Rapids, Mich.: Baker, 1987).

6. L. H. Ganong and M. Coleman, "Preparing for Remarriage: Anticipating the Issues, Seeking Solutions," *Family Relations* 38 (1989):28–33.

7. Ibid.

8. Stanley, S., "Trying Marriage Again," *Center for Marital and Family Studies Report*, Spring 1988:2.

9. Ganong and Coleman, "Preparing for Remarriage."

10. H. N. Wright, *Before You Remarry: A Guide to Successful Remarriage* (Eugene, Ore.: Harvest House, 1988).

11. L. Messinger, "Remarriage Between Divorced People with Children from Previous Marriages: A Proposal for Preparation for Remarriage," *Journal of Marriage and Family Counseling* 2 (1976):193–200; L. Messinger, L. Walker, and S. Freeman, "Preparation for Remarriage Following Divorce: The Use of Group Techniques," *American Journal of Orthopsychiatry* 48 (1978):263–72.

12. Ganong and Coleman, "Preparing for Remarriage."

Chapter 11 Principles for Preparing Individual Couples for Marriage

1. C. R. Rogers, "The Necessary and Sufficient Conditions of Therapeutic Personality Change," *Journal of Consulting Psychology* 21 (1957):95–103.

2. E. L. Worthington, Jr., *When Someone Asks for Help: A Practical Guide for Counseling* (Downers Grove, Ill.: InterVarsity Press, 1982).

3. M. Selvini-Palazzoli et al., *Paradox and Counterparadox* (New York: Jason Aronson, 1978).

4. D. H. Olson, D. G. Fournier, and J. M. Druckman, *PREPARE-ENRICH Counselors Manual*, rev. ed. (Stillwater, Okla.: PREPARE-ENRICH, 1980); D. G. Fournier, D. H. Olson, and J. M. Druckman, "The PREPARE-ENRICH Inventories," in E. E. Filsinger, ed., *A Sourcebook in Marriage and Family Assessment* (Beverly Hills, Calif.: Sage, 1983):229–50.

5. M. T. Schaefer and D. H. Olson, "Assessing Intimacy: The PAIR Inventory," *Journal of Marital and Family Therapy* 7 (1981).

6. R. F. Stahmann and W. J. Hiebert, *Premarital Counseling* (Lexington, Mass.: Lexington Books, 1980).

7. R. M. Taylor and L. P. Morrison, *Taylor-Johnson Temperament Analysis (T-JTA)* (Los Angeles: Psychological Publications, 1966–77).

8. K. Briggs and I. Myers, *Myers-Briggs Type Indicator, Form G,* (Palo Alto, Calif.: Consulting Psychologists Press, 1977); I. Briggs-

Myers and M. McCauley, *A Guide to the Development and Use of the Myers-Briggs Type Indicator* (Palo Alto, Calif.: Consulting Psychologists Press, 1985).

9. Stahmann and Hiebert, *Premarital Counseling*.

10. I prefer using the term "marital enrichment" to "neomarital counseling"; labeling the service as "counseling" will inhibit many couples from attending because they do not wish to admit publicly that they need counseling.

Chapter 12 Principles for Conducting Preparation-for-Marriage Groups

1. G. Corey, *Theory and Practice of Group Counseling* (Monterey, Calif.: Brooks/Cole, 1981); M. M. Ohlsen, *Marriage Counseling in Groups* (Champaign, Ill.: Research Press, 1979); D. S. R. Garland, *Working with Couples for Marriage Enrichment* (San Francisco: Jossey-Bass, 1983).

2. Corey, *Theory and Practice of Group Counseling*.

3. Ibid.

4. H. H. Strupp, S. W. Hadley, and B. Gomez-Schwartz, *Psychotherapy for Better or Worse* (New York: Jason Aronson, 1977).

Chapter 13 Modules for Marriage Preparation

1. D. S. R. Garland, *Working with Couples for Marriage Enrichment* (San Francisco: Jossey-Bass, 1983); M. M. Ohlsen, *Marriage Counseling in Groups* (Champaign, Ill.: Research Press, 1979).

2. R. F. Stahmann and W. J. Hiebert, *Premarital Counseling* (Lexington, Mass.: Lexington Books, 1980), 136–38.

3. J. Block, *The California Q-Set* (Form III) (Palo Alto, Calif.: Consulting Psychologists Press, 1978; adapted by D. Bem, 1978).

4. Garland, *Working with Couples;* M. M. Ohlsen, *Marriage Counseling in Groups*.

5. D. J. Rolfe, "Preparing the Previously Married for Second Marriage," *Journal of Pastoral Care* 39 (1985):110–19.

6. E. L. Worthington, Jr., *Marriage Counseling: A Christian Approach to Counseling Couples* (Downers Grove, Ill.: InterVarsity Press, 1989.

7. M. T. Schaefer and D. H. Olson, "Assessing Intimacy: The PAIR Inventory," *Journal of Marital and Family Therapy* 7 (1981).

8. Ibid.

9. Garland, *Working with Couples*, 256–57.

10. K. Guerin, "Engaging the Emotional Distances in Family Therapy," *The Family* 11, no. 1 (1983):13–17; P. K. Guerin, "The Stages of Marital Conflict," *The Family* 10, no. 1 (1982):15–26.

11. R. B. Stuart, *Helping Couples Change: A Social Learning Approach to Marital Therapy* (New York: Guilford, 1980).

12. N. S. Jacobson and G. Margolin, *Marital Therapy: Strategies Based on Social Learning and Behavior Exchange Principles* (New York: Brunner/Mazel, 1979).

13. J. Gottman et al., *A Couple's Guide to Communication* (Champaign, Ill.: Research Press, 1976), 189–200.

14. Ibid., 201–15.

15. Garland, *Working with Couples*, 271–72.

16. Worthington, *Marriage Counseling*.

17. Garland, *Working with Couples*, 250–51.

18. L. J. Crabb, Jr., *The Marriage Builder* (Grand Rapids, Mich.: Zondervan, 1982).

19. Stuart, *Helping Couples Change*.

20. Garland, *Working with Couples*, 261–62.

21. R. Fisher and W. Ury, *Getting to Yes: Negotiating Agreement Without Giving In* (New York: Penguin Books, 1981).

22. C. E. Rusbult, "A Longitudinal Test of the Investment Model: The Development (and Deterioration) of Satisfaction and Commitment in Heterosexual Involvement," *Journal of Personality and Social Psychology* 45 (1983): 101–17.

Chapter 14 Modules for Preparing Couples for Remarriage

1. M. McGoldrick and B. Carter, "Forming a Remarried Family" in Carter and McGoldrick, eds., *The Changing Family Life Cycle*; E. B. Visher and J. S. Visher, *Old Loyalties, New Ties: Therapeutic Strategies with Stepfamilies* (New York: Brunner/Mazel, 1988).

2. Visher and Visher, *Old Loyalties, New Ties*.

3. P. Papernow, "The Stepfamily Cycle: An Experiential Model of Stepfamily Development," *Family Relations* 33 (1984).

4. T. W. Roberts and S. J. Price, "Instant Families: Divorced Mothers Marry Never-Married Men," *Journal of Divorce* 11 (1987)."

5. E. L. Worthington, Jr., and B. G. Buston, "The Marriage Relationship in the Transition to Parenthood: A Review and a Model," *Journal of Family Issues* 7 (1986):443–73.

6. D. H. Olson et al., *Families: What Makes Them Work?* (Beverly Hills, Calif.: Sage, 1983).

INDEX

Everett L. Worthington, Jr., Ph.D.

Everett Worthington is associate professor of psychology at the Virginia Commonwealth University. He has authored numerous scholarly research articles and has written six books, including *When Someone Asks for Help, How to Help the Hurting, Marriage Counseling: A Christian Approach to Counseling Couples*, and *Counseling for Unplanned Pregnancy and Infertility*. Having received the B.S. at the University of Tennessee and the M.S. at Massachusetts Institute of Technology, both in nuclear engineering, he held a commission in the U.S. Navy and served as an instructor in the Naval Nuclear Power School. Dr. Worthington subsequently earned the M.A. and Ph.D. degrees in counseling psychology at the University of Missouri. He and his wife Kirby live in Richmond, Virginia, and are the parents of four children, Christen, Jonathan, Becca, and Katy Anna.